ADDED VALUE NEGOTIATING

NEGOTIATING

The Breakthrough Method for Building Balanced Deals

ADDED VALUE NEGOTIATING

The Breakthrough Method for Building Balanced Deals

Karl Albrecht

Steve Albrecht

BUSINESS ONE IRWIN
Homewood, Illinois 60430

Sponsoring editor:	Cynthia A. Zigmund
Project editor:	Stephanie M. Britt
Production manager:	Irene H. Sotiroff
Jacket designer:	Sam Concialdi
Art coordinator:	Heather Burbridge
Compositor:	BookMasters, Inc.
Typeface:	11/13 Times Roman
Printer:	Book Press, Inc.

Library of Congress Cataloging-in-Publication Data

Albrecht, Karl.
    Added value negotiating : the breakthrough method for building
balanced deals / by Karl Albrecht and Steve Albrecht.
        p.   cm.
    Includes index.
    ISBN 1-55623-967-X
    1. Negotiation in business.   2. Negotiation.   I. Albrecht,
Steven.   II. Title.
    HD58.6.A43   1993
    158'.5—dc20   92–43739

Printed in the United States of America
2 3 4 5 6 8 9 0 BP 0 9 8 7 6 5 4 3

Preface

All of us are negotiators at various times in our lives, whether we know it or not and whether we like it or not. While many people think of a negotiator as someone formally appointed to represent a country or a corporation in some matter of great importance, the truth is that most of the negotiations in the world happen on a much smaller scale.

We all have to make deals in various areas of our lives: getting a new job, getting a promotion, getting married, getting divorced, buying or selling property, renting an office or an apartment, getting involved in an investment, leasing a car, dealing with a labor union, settling a dispute between departments, or going into a business venture with someone else. Most of us negotiate much more often than we consciously realize.

Yet most of us are not very good negotiators. Negotiating isn't something most of us ever learn in any deliberate way. It seems to be something we're all supposed to pick up somewhere along the journey from childhood to adulthood.

Apparently, most people don't pick it up very well, at least judging by the negative feelings they seem to have about it. Women in particular often feel uncomfortable with the aggressive, male-oriented power tactics generally accepted as the norm in business negotiations. In the wider world of human beings, things don't seem to go very well either, judging by the troubles people and nations have getting along with one another. Just a few examples tell the tale.

California Governor Pete Wilson collided with his state legislature over key budget provisions. Wilson kept vetoing their submissions and they kept refusing to submit the budget he wanted. Result: the state government of California eventually ran out of funds and couldn't even pay its employees' salaries. For several months, the state ran on IOUs redeemable in the future at 5 percent interest.

In Australia, the airline pilots' union decided to strike for wage increases of 20 to 30 percent. Their tough negotiators faced off against the tough negotiators of the airline companies and the government, and the strike dragged on for months. Result: the government dissolved the union, but not before the economy came to a virtual standstill, tourism to Australia was in shreds, and hundreds of small companies that depended on tourism were driven to the wall.

American football star Joe Phillips played hardball with the owners of the San Diego Chargers team, refusing even to react to their offers until finally the owners invoked their privilege of benching him for an entire season. Result: he received no salary, couldn't break out of his contract with them, and they got no value from his talents.

Japan has an estimated 11 lawyers per 100,000 citizens. The United Kingdom has 82, Germany has 111, and the United States has 281. Clearly, some societies are more geared toward legal combat as a way of solving problems. Some cultures are more likely to see negotiating as a battle of wills or a battle of wits.

In recent years, some business people have begun to realize that the traditional idea of negotiation as a form of combat is seriously limited in its potential. The idea of presenting someone with an unfair offer and expecting him or her to counterattack with an equally unfair demand, on the presumption that the two parties can somehow fight their way to an acceptable middle ground, is becoming obsolete.

A new era, with new and more complex problems and issues, calls for new thinking. We are beginning to understand that negotiating is a complex social and psychological process that usually goes well beyond the basic economic proposition with which most people tend to start. It calls for a more skillful way of interacting, and a more thoughtful approach to balancing the interests of all parties. But we don't live in a win-win world yet.

Over the past decade or so, we have been working with a rather unusual negotiating method that we have evolved and tested extensively. We call this method *added value negotiating* (AVN). We have tried to draw upon the best ideas of effective negotiators whom we consider advocates of this new thinking process of adding value rather than extracting or conceding value. We have added several key aspects to create a method that is quite different from most methods currently in use.

Added value negotiating sets aside several of the most basic assumptions people have always made about how to make deals:

- Never make your best offer at the start.
- Never accept the other party's first demand; it's always higher than the one they will accept.

- Never make a concession without getting something equal or better in return.
- Try to discover the other side's weaknesses, and don't let them discover yours.
- Keep them guessing; don't tell them anything you don't have to.
- Get the upper hand early in the negotiation and keep it.

By adopting an entirely different ethical stance, it is possible to leave behind all of these psychologically primitive attitudes and their accompanying tactics, and approach a negotiation from the standpoint of adding value. We have seen abundant evidence that an attitude of openness and candor about interests, a willingness to give value rather than try to extract it, and a world view of abundance rather than scarcity can work wonders in bringing people to agreement.

One of the features that makes AVN so different from standard win-lose or even so-called win-win negotiating is the concept of multiple deals. Instead of offering one deal and hoping to beat it into shape, the AVN approach calls for the creation of multiple deal packages. It's much more comfortable psychologically for a person to choose among several alternatives than have to do battle from a fixed position. Because each deal package is based on a mutual understanding of interests and the options that can meet them, both sides get a sense that the negotiating process is both balanced and fair.

By applying these principles in the framework of a simple five-step method, and by structuring the possibilities with two simple planning worksheets (the window of interest and the option tree), it is possible to make more of your negotiations produce more fruitful results. At the same time you can build strong relationships of mutual respect and trust.

This is the prescription for added value negotiating that we have tried to develop in this book. It is not perfect, of course, and it will surely evolve and develop over time.

Some of what we have to say here may tax your credulity at first. Most of it, we believe, will begin to make sense once you explore the context of added value and begin to see how profoundly different it is from the standard win-lose approaches so common today. Ultimately, you will have to see whether these methods work in your own life. We have seen them work in ours.

Karl Albrecht
Steve Albrecht

Contents

Chapter Eight
GETTING TO THE HANDSHAKE
Perfecting the Deal   141

Chapter Nine
SOME FINAL THOUGHTS ON NEGOTIATING   158

This scorpion wanted to cross a river, so he asked the frog to carry him.

"No," said the frog, "no, thank you. If I let you on my back you may sting me, and the sting of the scorpion is death."

"Now, where," asked the scorpion, "is the logic of that?" (for scorpions always try to be logical). "If I sting you, you will die and I will drown."

So the frog was convinced, and allowed the scorpion on his back. But just in the middle of the river he felt a terrible pain and realized that, after all, the scorpion had stung him.

"Logic!" cried the dying frog as he started under, bearing the scorpion down with him. "There is no logic in this!"

"I know," said the scorpion, "but I can't help it—it's my character."

Orson Welles, Mr. Arkadin

Chapter One

Head-Butting 101
The Way We've Always Done It

"Our talks were exceedingly cordial and fruitful. In other words, we are at war."

HOW NOT TO WIN A CONTRACT—
BY KARL ALBRECHT

About 20 years ago, while I was employed as a technical marketing manager with a California aerospace firm, I first started thinking seriously about the problem of how human beings negotiate. I had an unsuccessful experience as a negotiator for my company that had a profound effect on my thinking about how people and companies do business.

That experience has lurked in the background of my mind all these years, and has occasionally nibbled away at my consciousness. It eventually led me to conclude that the entire Western mindset of negotiating in business is deeply flawed and much in need of a better way of thinking.

My job was to lead the "capture team" for my company in competing for a multimillion dollar contract with the U.S. Defense Department. We had enjoyed the dominant market position in this particular area of defense systems development for years, but for various reasons it was necessary for us to join up with a suitable partner and bid for the project as part of a team of contractors.

We were in this predicament because we had picked up signals through market intelligence that the senior officials of the Defense agency considered us too successful and too dominant, and intended to open up the playing field to our competitors. If we were to bid for the project as prime contractor, we would surely not be selected. Our only hope was to join forces with another strong company, put them in the role of prime contractor, and take a background role as a support contractor. My job was to find a suitable joint venture partner and negotiate the terms of the relationship.

We had narrowed the field to two possible partners, Company A and Company B. Both had good reputations, but Company A was so well qualified technically that they were the obvious choice. But there was a hitch: they were also one of our toughest competitors in other areas of the market, and our relationship with them was not very cordial.

Nevertheless, there were compelling reasons for forming a partnership with Company A. In fact, our intelligence suggested that if the two companies could field a competitive team, most of the other likely competitors would probably drop out. Our chances of winning the project would be better than 90 percent, which is very high in the aerospace business.

I was under considerable pressure from my management to do two things: one, to get the deal, and two, to secure the upper hand in the relationship so that we, not they, would actually be guiding the project and receiving most of the revenue. The clock was ticking; we had to choose a partner quickly to get the proposal together and deliver it to the government.

After preliminary contacts with Company A, things looked promising. We scheduled a summit meeting. This meeting took place in our fortress, with their executives visiting us. The spokesperson for their team was my counterpart, the marketing man charged with negotiating their side of the deal.

Imagine the situation: My counterpart, Mr. A, and I were seated across from each other at a large conference table. His vice presidents were seated behind him. My vice presidents were seated behind me. Both of us were under the age of thirty, and both were relatively inexperienced negotiators.

After the usual gestures of hospitality, we got right down to the negotiating. Mr. A presented his proposal. It was so skewed in their favor as to be a virtual slap in the face to our company. He proposed to relegate us to a very minor role, with a very small share of the revenue.

I expressed the suitable degree of outrage and counterattacked with a proposal that was just as skewed in our direction. Then he expressed outrage and defended his original position. Now we were in a stalemate, both technically and psychologically.

Both of us were under pressure to show our respective bosses that we were not wimps, so we stood our ground. We both proved we were "tough negotiators." The discussion degenerated to verbal fisticuffs, with each of us showing the other how tough he was.

It became clear that the gulf between our positions was horribly wide. At one point, one of Company A's vice presidents intervened and offered a major concession from their position. One of my vice presidents intervened, pocketed that concession, and demanded a concession in a related technical area. This caused the other vice president to balk. After a few minutes of awkward silence, someone suggested that we adjourn the meeting, retire to our respective castles, and give the matter some further thought. We would get together again in a day or two to resume the talks.

The next morning, the chief executive of my company received a telephone call from the chief of Company A, saying, in effect, "Go to hell." They had decided to compete for the contract head-on against us. As a result, we had no choice but to form a relationship with Company B, our second choice.

After a long and costly competition, we lost the bid for the contract. Company A won. Our only consolation was that, without our technical expertise to draw on, they lost their shirt as the costs got completely out of hand.

There was a bitter lesson for all involved: Had we reached an effective agreement, the two companies could have won the contract hands-down and both would have made a profit. It wasn't a win-win affair. It wasn't even a win-lose affair. It was a lose-lose affair all around.

Mr. A and I had both used the standard approach of tough negotiators, that is, the macho, power-oriented, push-and-shove, demand-and-concede form of combat widely accepted in the business world, and certainly widely accepted among males. We all lost. I felt guilty about it. I felt that I had failed. I had been tough, but we didn't get the contract. I suppose that he also felt bad. Many times after that, I wondered how we might have avoided the deadlock and made a deal.

HOW NOT TO SELL A BUSINESS— BY STEVE ALBRECHT

Fear can be a powerful motivator but decisions made out of fear have a nasty way of coming back to haunt you. In business, fear-based choices usually spring from money issues. I had a personal experience that taught me a lot about negotiating in a state of fear and apprehension.

Some years ago I was faced with a number of difficult tasks revolving around the impending sale of my small client-service business. My morale had reached a low ebb, thanks to a bitter feud with my partner. As is often the case in these business divorce situations, our animosity centered on money. Our relationship had deteriorated to a point where we could hardly speak to each other on the phone, let alone sit in the same room.

In this context of mistrust and anger, I tried to arrange for the sale of our business to an interested party. Selling a business is never an easy process and bad feelings among the owners only make a nerve-wracking situation worse. Besides arranging the financial papers and trying to solicit potential buyers, I was also saddled with the day-to-day operations of running the business.

In between putting out the countless client "brush fires," collecting past-due accounts, and doing the work itself, I was able to schedule a meeting with a man who owned a business like ours and appeared interested in expanding his client base.

I had heard that this gentleman had a reputation of being a tough negotiator. His East Coast background, flair for overly dramatic advertising campaigns, and questionable reputation among his past clients made me leery. Because the clock was ticking and I wanted to pursue other business opportunities, I decided to do my research and to present "Mr. Tough" with a detailed plan for the sale of my company. After a few eerily short phone conversations, I set an appointment with Mr. Tough for the following Friday.

Discussions with some of my associates in this business area left me feeling more than a bit apprehensive about the approaching meeting. When one of my associates said in a not-so-delicate manner, "He's a ball-buster," I prepared for the worst. As much as I told myself to put on my own tough-negotiator face, I couldn't shake the feeling that I wanted and needed this man to buy my business. Regardless of my personal feelings toward him, I told myself, it will serve my interests best if he agrees to my deal, even if I have to put up with some grief from him in the process.

On the appointed day, I drove to the heart of San Diego's commercial business district, parked in a well-known high-rise building, and took the elevator up to the 20th floor. Stepping inside a huge, oak-paneled foyer, I gave my name to the secretary, sat down, and waited for Mr. Tough to see me . . . and waited . . . and waited . . . and waited some more.

When Mr. Tough thought I had cooled my heels on his couch long enough, he buzzed his secretary to take me back to his office. As I met him at the door, I saw but did not recognize the usual trappings of a typical power negotiator. As I sat in the chair across from his big desk, my eyes fell upon the wall behind him. What I first thought might be a rolling advertisement for a picture frame store turned out to be a collection of every diploma, certificate, plaque, and merit badge that Mr. Tough had garnered during his business career. I barely had time to take in the commanding skyline view of the city, the seven-foot desk, and the bank of important-looking phones at his side.

Lighting the first of many cigarettes, Mr. Tough shared what he thought was an amusing story about how he and my erstwhile partner had insulted each other upon their first meeting several years ago.

As I stammered my way through an embarrassed reply, he picked up a copy of our client list and said, "I'm not too impressed with these clients. Only one firm on this whole list is worth anything. The rest are just small-timers. I'm only interested in the big name here."

He then threw out a price for the sale of the business that was 25 percent of the original price that we had discussed in letters and phone conversations.

While he let this new piece of news sink in, he began playing a version of the ever-popular game called "Who do you know?" This common conversational trick offers a way for two unfamiliar parties to gauge each other by their respective friends, peers, enemies, mentors, or associates. While I usually enjoy playing this game because it helps me to establish common ground, Mr. Tough took great delight in making pointed comments about my friends and associates, that is, "He's a jerk," "I know that cheapskate," and so on.

As the meeting progressed (or sank), I became aware of an incredible urge to bolt from the room. Mr. Tough sat smoking and taking careful aim at my already bruised ego with his remarks about the relative ill health of my business, my experience in the business, and the quality of my work. In between his diatribes, which were always spoken with a big Cheshire-like smile on his face, he would take "important" phone calls from his secretary and let slip to her information like the cost of his monthly phone bill (more than my biweekly salary) and the names of some of his VIP clients.

By the end of the meeting he had nearly convinced me that my business was not worth what I—the owner—said it was; that most of my client list was not worth his time; and that it was probably good that I was getting out of the business because guys like him were going to take over the whole town anyway. He also whittled down his original offer to an even more microscopic figure and had the nerve to ask me, "So, do we have a deal or what?" as he showed me to the door. I smiled weakly, promised to call him later, and limped to the elevator.

Driving home from the encounter, I experienced the most complex set of emotions I'd ever felt. I could have given an authentic Academy Award performance: I could have laughed, cried, bellowed in rage, screamed, or sulked in an instant. My meeting with Mr. Tough had proved one thing: He truly was a power negotiator and I wasn't.

As I discussed that horrible day with the much more agreeable man to whom I eventually sold the business two months later, I recalled my head-first baptism into the tricks and tactics of so-called power negotiators:

1. Make them meet you on your turf; have them come to your office, your city, or your country.

2. Intimidate them with all of the trappings of power outside your office (big building, big elevators, big waiting rooms, big furniture, a secretary/shield).

3. Let 'em wait. You're a busy person. You have important things to do and this little meeting is just one of many things on your power-packed daily agenda.

4. Show off your accomplishments. Those plaques, certificates, and diplomas tell everyone you're a power broker who has paid some heavy dues and has the rewards to prove it.

5. Put them in front of your big, imposing desk. Make them sit in hardback chairs while you relax in your comfy padded number.

6. Go ahead and smoke if you feel like it. If your cigarettes make them feel uncomfortable, queasy, or distracted, all the better. Better for your lungs and bloodstream to feel content than to worry about their breathing problems.

7. Don't let this little meeting interfere with your normal business operations. Take those important calls during the session; there is no sense in making your real clients or employees wait.

8. Talk badly about their partners, clients, and fellow associates. After all, it's a tough world out there and you know best about who really calls the shots around town.

9. Drive their offer down right away. Make an immediate counter-offer and show them you won't be fooled by a stack of spread-sheets, cost estimates, and revenue expectations. Come in low and dig lower. What can it hurt?

10. Finally, act like you're doing them a favor just by having them come to your office and listening to their pitch. Make it seem like you're doing them an even bigger favor and offer to take everything off their hands for a fair (to you) price.

If any or all of these tactics sound familiar to you, you're not alone. Chances are good that you've run across this type of power negotiator during your business and personal dealings. I was fortunate enough to run into this person early in my business career. I learned a great deal from the encounter but I still have a few psychological scars from the battle.

DEAL OR DUEL: THE PSYCHOLOGICAL DILEMMA OF NEGOTIATING

For some years after the episodes just described, and following some others much like them, we have reflected on the fundamental question of negotiation: Is it a form of combat between two parties, with each striving to get the better of the other, or is it a form of cooperation that seeks a balance of both interests?

We human beings suffer from an anxious ambivalence in our thinking about negotiating. One part of us wants to play fair, create good will, and be honest and forthright. Another part of us is afraid of being taken, manipulated, or pushed into agreeing to something we don't understand or don't feel good about. Most people seem to suffer a sense of uncertainty and confusion about this incredibly personal and psychological process.

After reading a number of books and articles on negotiating and attending a number of seminars on the subject over the years, we have concluded that most people can't answer the question for themselves in a very satisfying way. Most of the books, articles, and seminars tout a win-win approach, but in fact present all sorts of combative and manipulative methods to help you get one up on your opponent. The terminology of the advertising brochure is reassuring, but the terminology of the actual approach reveals a very different mindset.

The savvy consultant writing the article in the business magazine or newsletter tells you to approach the negotiation with a win-win philosophy. Then he gives you a trick: Try to get your opponent to travel to your home city and call an early-morning meeting so he or she will be suffering from jet lag and won't be operating at peak mental efficiency. It's a strange, self-contradictory message.

You're supposed to consider the other person's interests, but at the same time the writer advises you to focus your premeeting research on discovering the other person's weaknesses. How can you get the opponent over a barrel? What weakness, need, or hang-up does he or she have that you can exploit?

The book talks about negotiating as a process of meeting the interests of both parties, and then instructs you to observe the other person's body language for cues that reveal his actual intentions. One book we reviewed knowingly revealed:

> If the other person won't look you in the eye when he speaks, or kicks his foot or rubs his neck, he's probably not telling the truth.

Several highly publicized gurus of negotiating training offer their own unique but questionable interpretations of the meanings of various isolated unconscious gestures taken out of their cultural and psychological context. Even if accurate, which they're probably not, these gimmicky diagnoses tend to contradict the spirit of cooperation that they profess to profess.

In a typical article in an executive newsletter, the author offers five principles of negotiating:

1. Make your negotiating opponent fully aware of your power.
2. Try to discover early your opponent's motives for every negotiating position/action.
3. Effectively use language, both spoken and written.
4. Recite facts and let others draw their own conclusions.
5. Control or influence the ground rules and the agenda.

Note the use of terms like opponent, power, control, motives, and influence.

With all of this ambiguity and self-contradiction surrounding the subject of negotiating, it's no wonder so many people are ambivalent about it. Is it combat? Is it cooperation? Is it combat disguised as cooperation? Is the basic trick simply to make your opponent think it's cooperation, while you zap him with your various clever tactics?

This is the question we need to answer for ourselves. The answer to the question goes to the very bottom of your personal values as a human being. For our part, we have answered it. We believe a negotiation should be a cooperation. There is no real joy in life from getting the better of others. Those who need to appear superior are not truly happy people. There is no joy in feeling that you've been beaten by a tough negotiator. We believe there is a zone of satisfaction between the two extremes, based on the concept of *added value*.

We don't believe a person always has to choose between taking others and being taken. There is a better choice. We believe it is possible, desirable, and rewarding to negotiate deals that bring value to all parties and that it is possible to do so without psychological suffering in most cases. The key is in combining three factors: empathy, fairness, and assertiveness. It involves much more than just mouthing the platitudes of win-win. It involves learning methods for analyzing value and constructing deals that appeal. This is the method we propose to develop for you in this book.

PULLING TEETH: NEGOTIATING AS EXTRACTING CONCESSIONS

There is a strange psychology that seems to set in during the most aggressive kinds of negotiations in which people are bent on showing each

other how tough they are. When egos get involved, when people take
firm positions, and when each sees the other as either an opponent to be
conquered or a predator to be fended off, value becomes reductive rather
than additive. As the deal progresses—if, indeed, it does—it is more
likely to shrink than to grow, in terms of the total payoff for both sides.

This happens because people who operate from a psychological stance
of competitiveness, defensiveness, fear, or anger tend to retreat to a
taking-withholding mode of behavior rather then a giving-sharing mode.

This is why many of the standard win-lose negotiating manuals devote a
great deal of attention to the topic of concessions. Specifically, they counsel the reader to avoid giving them and to try hard to get them. The very
choice of the term signals an attitude of scarcity, reluctance, and withholding—a zero-sum view of the value involved in the situation. You
only get what the other side gives up; what they get is what you give up.

The typical Western view considers negotiation to begin when one
party makes the other an offer. The next step is for the second party to
reject the offer as insufficient and to make a counteroffer. This offer-
counteroffer reflex is about as old as human beings. It is at the very core
of business thinking. We all know that the other party will never make
the best and final offer right off the bat. The counteroffer will, presumably, be less generous than what they are actually willing to settle on.
Knowing this, we must, of course, counter with something lower and less
generous than what we are willing to settle on.

Then, according to ancient and unwritten law, the real negotiation begins. If the two parties are to arrive at an agreement under these circumstances, it must certainly be less valuable to both of them than the deals
they originally proposed. By definition, the only way they can arrive at
consensus is for either or both of them to make concessions from their
original positions.

Real estate purchases, for example, especially for homes, tend to follow a cut-and-dried pattern of negotiating. Coached by two realtors, the
prospective buyer and prospective seller engage in a formal dance of offer and counteroffer that ends up at a selling price both realtors can predict within a few percentage points' variation. This "mortgage minuet"
starts with an asking price almost ten percent above the market price for
similar homes in the area. The buyer counters with an offer about ten
percent below the market value. The realtors dutifully exchange offers,
each advising his or her client that the other side probably won't concede
the whole difference.

After two or three times around the dance floor, they usually end up splitting the difference between the first asking price and the first counteroffer. The final price point might vary a bit according to some related considerations, but usually it's pretty close to the price the realtors had in mind to begin with.

Because of this highly programmed ritual, most home sales are really not negotiations, other than in name. Most often, buyer and seller are strangers and never get to know one another. Neither knows anything about the other's life, problems, or interests, and so neither is in a position to discuss any elements of possible value in the deal except the price. There may be a few token items pushed back and forth, but these usually serve only to create the impression that there has been a negotiation and to help each party conclude that his or her realtor really contributed enough to justify the commission.

You can hear business people talking about the outcomes of negotiations with other businesses, for example: "Well, we got X and we got Y, but we didn't get Z"; "We had to give up A to get them to go along with B." It is the language of capturing and losing territory; the language of extracting and yielding concessions.

The added value negotiating concept offers the possibility that, by focusing on value itself, not on concessions, it is usually possible to enrich the deal for both sides, which makes it additive rather than reductive. This is the origin of the very name of the method. By postponing the making of offers until we understand the common and disparate interests of both sides, we can find ways to add in different forms of value.

By proposing several different types of deals, all relatively balanced for both sides, we can eliminate the offer and counteroffer form of implied combat and focus on finding consensus. In the best of circumstances, we can end up with deals that surpass the initial hopes of both parties, because the open-minded and creative search for value turns up unexpected possibilities.

MAKING THEM SAY "UNCLE": DO YOU WANT TO BE A TOUGH NEGOTIATOR?

In the arena of international politics, it is usually a high form of flattery to refer to someone as a tough negotiator. Henry Kissinger is often described as a tough negotiator. At the height of the arms race talks, the

Soviets were described frequently as tough negotiators. Israelis and most Arabs are usually thought to be tough negotiators.

What does being a tough negotiator mean? Basically, it seems to mean that people can't get much out of you. You are a person who stands your ground, makes very few concessions, and eventually gets what you want. Being tough means that you rarely bend, offer little without getting more back, and generally exhibit all of the mobility, flexibility, generosity, and openness of a park statue.

Being a tough negotiator means you don't surrender, you don't concede, and you don't give up anything without getting something of equal or greater value in return. It seems to be more a definition of what you don't do than what you do.

What happens when two tough negotiators deal with each other? The answer: not much. Study the history of international negotiations handled by tough negotiators and you'll see that they make progress very slowly, if at all. Treaties on arms limitations between the United States and the former Soviet Union took years to develop. Decades passed without substantial progress between Israel and its Arab neighbors.

When representatives of the United States and North Vietnam met in Paris to discuss the ceasefire, it took them several weeks of tough negotiating to settle the issue of the size and shape of the table around which they would meet. Meanwhile, the people of their countries continued killing one another in Vietnam.

In recent years, tough negotiators from the United States and Japan have met to improve trade relations but experience very slow progress. Trade delegations sent to Japan, including the infamous Bush tour, in which George Bush took the chief executives of several distressed American companies to present their demands, have been met with bows, inscrutable smiles, and almost no significant concessions.

In Australia, the airline pilots' union decided several years ago to strike for wage raises of 20 to 30 percent. Their tough negotiators faced off against the tough negotiators of the airline companies and the government: the strike dragged on for months. Finally, the government dissolved the union, but not before the economy came to a virtual standstill. Tourism to Australia was in shreds, and hundreds of small companies that depended on tourism were driven to the wall.

Two tough negotiators on opposite sides of an issue are likely to end up with a fairly minimal deal. Each side intends to win while expecting that the other side will lose, or at least not gain as much. In reality, during a hard-fought win-lose negotiating battle, both sides often come out with little more than a shell of a deal, much less than they might have gained had they engaged in a mutual search for value. They start with an offer and a counteroffer and spend the rest of their time whittling each other down.

We're not at all sure being a tough negotiator is a good thing. We suggest, rather, that one strive to be an *effective* negotiator. The differences between the two are notable.

Tough negotiators are not always obnoxious people. Some of them are outwardly pleasant, cordial, and engaging, but inwardly crafty, calculating, and determined. The proverbial car salesman is probably the quintessence of the friendly but tough negotiator, perhaps admired by some as much as loathed by others.

For many people, the process of buying a new car ranks somewhere between root canal surgery by using posthole diggers and walking barefoot on hot coals. They view car salespeople as being manipulative, sometimes arrogant, and overly aggressive. They dislike the confrontational negotiating atmosphere, and they often feel like they've been psychologically abused after the whole thing is over.

The reputation of the entire automobile industry rises and falls on the quality of their cars, but often the people at the frontlines, the sales force, are the weakest links to the customer. Abuses ranging from the hard sell to outright lies and deception seem to be more the rule than the exception.

We recall an incident in which two business people bought matching company cars for their business. They had some questions about how to register the new cars with the Department of Motor Vehicles, e.g. in their names or the company name. The salesman told them, "It's easy. You just fill out a few forms and pay the registration fees. We'll take care of the rest."

What he failed to mention was that the DMV would ask for one set of papers for each car and the leasing company would ask for something completely different, not to mention a "small" $500 title transfer fee for *each* car.

Our friends were justifiably outraged that the salesman had failed to explain this part of the registration laws to them. When they tried to complain to the dealership, they were told that the salesman no longer worked for the firm.

These kinds of stories plague the automotive industry like few others. Thanks to past bad experiences, many people see the process of buying a car as one rigged against them. They don't like to negotiate with the so-called sharks that seem to gravitate toward the profession. On the rare occasion that the process does go smoothly (e.g., no hidden costs for floormats tacked on at the end) they are both relieved and surprised at their good fortune.

Another definition of the tough negotiator, and probably a more accurate one, is the power negotiator. What defines the power negotiator is his or her desire to defeat the other party in some way, as a basic part of the proposition of negotiating. Whether this arises from a psychological drive or from an interpretation of his or her needs and circumstances, winning becomes more important than the deal itself.

We're reminded of a colleague who has published several books in his chosen professional field. He is well known in his area and highly regarded as an expert. Yet for all of his books that counsel people to go for the human side of any business relationship, he fails to heed his own advice.

In his negotiations with his book publishers, he makes frequent and outrageous demands during the contract talks, after the contract has been signed (better known as "the afterbite"), and after the book reaches the stores. Does the publisher give in to most of his hard-fought requests? In some cases, they do. Does the publisher offer him another book publishing contract for his future projects? They do not.

Power negotiators see the negotiation process as a contest, not a search for mutual gain. For this reason, they focus on power tactics, interpersonal dynamics, tricks, and tactics. They seek an unbalanced settlement, the more unbalanced in their favor, the better.

Power negotiators may exhibit a wide range of behavior patterns. Some are openly aggressive, domineering, and even belligerent; others may be more civilized but no less demanding and pushy; yet others may be more subtle, disguising their aims under a contrived pleasant demeanor. The objective is the same: to win more than you do.

Later chapters deal further with the interpersonal styles, behaviors, and tactics of the power negotiator. If this approach appeals to you, you will probably not find the remainder of the book very much to your liking. On the other hand, if your personal ethics require you to consider the humanity of others when dealing with them, we believe you will find much to agree with in the added value negotiating method.

PSYCHOLOGICAL BLOCKS TO NEGOTIATING

Why a person may feel apprehensive about negotiating has much to do with the psychology behind it. Many people, virtually all but the most aggressive power negotiators, report remarkably similar feelings about the prospect of working their way through a typical business deal or any other deal that involves possible high-stakes outcomes.

Certain natural reflexes, or emotional blocks, can hinder your ability to get a good deal for yourself. Take a look at the following list of psychological blocks to negotiating and see if you recognize some of them in yourself.

The need to be nice. Nobody wants the other party to go away mad. The power negotiator knows this and may pretend to pack up his briefcase and storm out of the room just so you'll agree to some large concession and not ruffle his feathers. Because the majority of us don't like conflict, this need to be nice may cause us to settle for less just to avoid trouble.

The need to be accepted and approved. This starts from childhood, where we always strived to fit in, to receive strokes from our parents, family, friends, and peers. Giving up large chunks of value in a negotiation just to have the other party say that you are a good person or a team player is another way in which people compromise their own needs.

The fear of confrontation, conflict, or disharmony. Conflict at the negotiating table raises everyone's blood pressure, and because many people abhor raised voices, they will concede to prevent a nose-to-nose confrontation with the other side. Power negotiators know how to make some people feel uncomfortable with aggressive, bullying tactics that make them appear larger than life.

Guilt about asserting your self-interest. Some people, perhaps most, have not bought into the "I'm okay–you're okay" theory as yet. It's quite possible that their personality style or their upbringing refuses to let them gain or win anything in a negotiation. Asking for too much money, too many items of value, or anything else, no matter how modest, may make them feel like they're cheating or they're getting more than they're entitled to on some unseen scorecard. Power negotiators may use the old guilt trip tactic to keep the timid souls down.

The fear of being taken.   This one is prevalent in people who have been through hard win-lose negotiating battles before. Their cheeks may still be red and their eyes a bit watery from the last ordeal. Because they're so worried about getting the shaft, they make it nearly impossible for other people to negotiate honestly with them. They think everyone has a hidden agenda and is out to take them again.

Being intimidated by domineering people.   Shy, reserved folks who face a negotiating situation with a bullying power negotiator are already behind the success curve. The power talker will know how to hit the right personality button to put the shy person back into his or her shell. Using hooded insults to their intelligence, a foreboding physical presence, or any of the well-known negotiating power traps and tactics, the power person can beat the shy one and get the best deal just by sheer psychological force.

Lack of self-confidence.   Low self-esteem plagues many people; even those who do a good job of hiding it with false bravado. Ploys by a power negotiator to undermine the other party's sense of self-worth or influence can cause them to give away many concessions just to get the whole event over with.

The difficulty of thinking under pressure.   Stress can interfere with our capacity to think on our feet. People are always telling police officers and firefighters, "I don't know how you do it. If that was me, I think I'd just freeze up." The power negotiator may throw many issues at the other party and ask him or her to make a number of immediate decisions, hoping he or she will make a judgment error in the process.

The prospect of negotiator's remorse.   Just as someone who purchases a major item can get a case of buyer's remorse, that is, "Did I make the right decision? Did I pay too much?" people involved in difficult negotiations may leave the table thinking, "Did I get a good deal?

Did I get hoodwinked?'' This is common when you feel unsure of yourself, the other party, or the value of the deal you just closed.

Fear of losing face with boss or colleagues. This is a distinct possibility if you work in a highly competitive business environment, where many people look over your shoulder. If you're about to negotiate a heavy-duty deal, the added pressure from your superiors or coworkers can make you reluctant to act or make you more aggressive than you originally planned.

Before you start flogging yourself for any of these feelings, rest assured that most of them are quite common and perfectly understandable, given the often tense environments that surround many negotiations. One of the best ways to alleviate many of these blocks is to recognize them before you begin any negotiation. If you know going in that you may encounter these feelings, you can give yourself a quick pep talk and know that you can still negotiate a deal to completion even if you feel some normal apprehension.

Before you can help the other person get a good deal, you have to help yourself first. Know what you want before you even go to the bargaining table. If you're open and honest, and you convey an attitude that says you're there to engage in a mutual search for value and not out to take unfair advantage, the other person will sense it and may come around more than he or she had originally planned.

HOW WE LEARN TO NEGOTIATE

Much of the style and psychology with which human beings approach the prospect of a negotiation comes from deep-lying feelings and attitudes they acquired in their early years. Most of us have had experiences of conflict, competition, and scarcity. When Mom gave us one piece of cake to share, and appointed one of us to cut it and allowed the other to choose the first slice, we learned some important things. Depending on the sibling relationship, we might have seen the task as making sure the other kid didn't get more than we did, just as much as making sure we got as much as possible. That one little experience, recapitulated thousands of times in our young lives in thousands of other ways, made us the negotiators we are.

Most of us gradually evolved this double-barreled notion of negotiating as getting as much as possible and preventing the other person from getting more than necessary. For most people, this stance is reinforced many times over in school, home life, and eventually in work life.

For a growing number of working people, there are even formal training programs on the subject of negotiating. More and more companies are either providing in-house training programs on the subject or sending employees to public seminars and workshops. This is probably a worthwhile trend, but too many of the training programs put on today still focus on the old win-lose approaches and fail to capitalize on the possibilities inherent in a more psychologically healthy focus on mutual value.

The accepted training approaches now prevalent in business fall into three categories, with the first two being by far the most common. They are win-lose, disguised win-lose, and true win-win. Let's review each of them.

Win-Lose Negotiating

This is the standard approach to the subject. Each party takes a position and sticks to it. Typically, there is an atmosphere of combat, power struggles, and adversarial relations. Agreement is reached, if at all, through a battle-of-wits process of extracting and yielding concessions. This is fundamentally a reductive process, that is, each party wants to give as little as possible to the other.

One side makes an offer and then the two sides spend their time hashing it out. The Arab-Israeli and U.S.-Soviet diplomatic struggles fall into this win-lose category, as do many labor union–management struggles, buyer-seller deals, and many negotiations that involve personality conflicts, power-based problems, or overt aggressiveness.

When you read articles in the business press about negotiating, you tend to see the same fare: usually a collection of tips about how to get the upper hand, but still operate under the guise of an alleged win-lose format.

Other helpful tips include creating a highly intimidating meeting location; putting more people on your side than they have on their side so you outnumber them; waiting until the other side has already returned home before you call to make changes in the not-so-final agreement, and so forth.

These are techniques unrelated to the value of the deal being exchanged. These so-called innovative, situational, contextual, power techniques are really just the same as the old techniques. It's still the same win-lose approach, whether it's disguised, blatant, or in-between.

The key elements of win-lose negotiating are as follows:

1. Each side adopts a position.
2. Concessions get extracted or surrendered.
3. An atmosphere of combat or psychological warfare exists.
4. Compromises come by giving up something.
5. Most of the negotiation centers around one-shot, one-price haggling.
6. The vocabulary and terminology used by each side revolves around battle, aggression, and, with males, sports metaphors.
7. The postnegotiation feelings usually have one happy party and one not-so-happy party; sometimes both are unhappy, and rarely are both happy.

Win-Lose Negotiating in Disguise

Contrasted to the straight win-lose approach, this approach adopts a pretense of cooperation with the other party, but the underlying tactics still come from an adversarial mindset. Terms like win-win negotiating are contradicted by terms like opponent, strategy, battleplan, tactics, and defense. In most cases, the terminology and vocabulary give this approach away.

The insidious mindset of the disguised win-lose approach is "I will win more than you, but you won't know it until later." A veteran of many corporate negotiations once wryly observed, "With the win-lose type you know exactly what happened to you. With the disguised win-lose approach, you figure it out on the plane going home."

As an example, the disguised win-lose artist may chat you up in the beginning of a negotiation by saying, "I believe in win-win negotiating," "We're all going to get rich with this deal," "I'm a straight shooter," and so on. Then they turn right around and use the techniques of win-lose on you anyway. The difference is that they disguise their approach, rather than coming at you full force like a typical power negotiator. They like to use the appearance of fair play, honesty, and candor as a way to distract you before they try to stick it to you during the actual negotiation.

These are the key elements of the disguised win-lose negotiating approach:

1. The positions are often invisible or hard to detect.
2. Secrecy, game-playing, and manipulation are the rules of the encounter.
3. There is an appearance of concessions.
4. There is an appearance of compromises.
5. There is an element of disguised combat, although the vocabulary or terminology usually gives it away.
6. The postnegotiation feelings usually leave one side feeling cheated, although not always immediately.
7. Feelings of negotiator's remorse (or "Why did I let that happen to me?") may set in later.

In terms of the way negotiating is handled in corporate and public seminars, there is the standard win-lose approach and then there is the new and original—win-lose-in-disguise approach. The latter is supposed to be more sophisticated, but it's just as intellectually corrupt as the straight win-lose approach.

The disguised win-lose approach simply tries to make the negotiator feel less guilty but it is not too long before the negotiator reverts back to the straight win-lose approach. In these seminars, they discuss how to read body language, how to decipher anxiety signals, how to use neuro-linguistic programming to interpret and manipulate emotional states, and how to discover weaknesses based on what people say or how they approach the process of negotiation.

True Win-Win Negotiating

Could it be possible to make the cake bigger rather than fight over the size of each person's slice? What if, instead of contending for position in a grab for fixed resources, the parties devoted their attention to expanding the value available to them? In such a case, the middle zone of agreement would be a better place for both. This is the possibility we shall explore as we proceed.

We hesitate even to use the term win-win negotiating because it has so often been used fraudulently in business and in negotiating training programs. If patriotism is the last refuge of a scoundrel, then win-win negotiating is the last refuge of the manipulator. The win-win context of cooperative deal building is perfectly feasible, but it requires a special combination of attitudes, values, self-esteem, and assertiveness that many people don't have in large measure. Probably more people use it as a pretext for manipulating others than in a true cooperative spirit.

In recent years, however, we have seen a small but growing school of thinking in business and in international affairs focused on *nonpositional negotiating*. This is the proposition that *what* is right counts for more than *who* is right. Traditional positional bargaining casts two protagonists as adopting positions that offer certain things and demand certain things at the outset, and with each trying to move the other off position without budging himself. Nonpositional negotiating concentrates on the merits of various proposals at hand.

The Harvard Negotiation Project, for example, which has been in existence since the 1970s, has been one of the primary centers of research and advocacy for negotiating "on the merits," as experts there call it. The landmark book *Getting to Yes,* published in 1981 by Roger Fisher and William Ury, presented one of the first major departures from standard win-lose thinking.

In our research and development of the added value negotiating method, we discovered the work of the Harvard Project after we had formulated our basic model. Although the AVN approach follows a different course of action than the Harvard method, nevertheless we believe the Harvard approach is an important breakthrough in negotiating, and one that is in perfect alignment philosophically with AVN.

According to Fisher and Ury:

> The answer to the question of whether to use soft positional bargaining or hard is "neither." Change the game. At the Harvard Negotiation Project we have been developing an alternative to positional bargaining: a method of negotiation explicitly designed to produce wise outcomes efficiently and amicably. This method, called *principled negotiation* or *negotiation on the merits,* can be boiled down to four basic points: people, interests, options, and criteria.

Many of the basic concepts of the AVN model come from the same ethical stance as that used by the Harvard model; consequently, much of our terminology is similar. Although we have high praise for the Harvard work, we believe it lacks several critical elements that we feel are necessary to give most people a comfortable approach to negotiating that they can use with minimal training.

The fundamental contrast between traditional negotiating and this new added value way of thinking is illustrated by Figure 1–1. The conventional win-lose or disguised win-lose approach works by putting the parties in opposition to each other. Each tries to minimize the value the

FIGURE 1–1

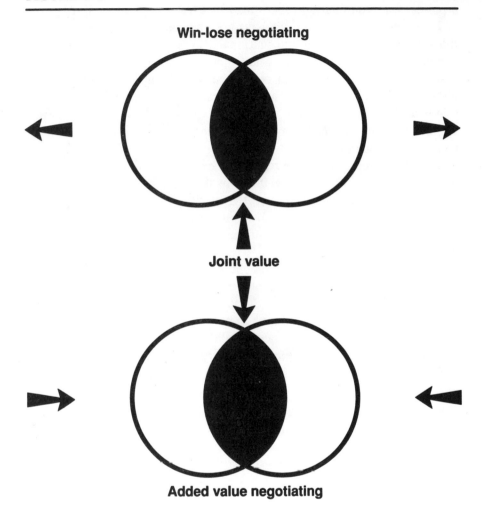

Win-lose negotiating

Joint value

Added value negotiating

other can extract from the deal. Of course, the process is reciprocal, so both parties are pulling apart. This results in their minimizing the total value between them, as represented by the overlapping area between the two circles.

Added value negotiating, on the other hand, works by figuratively pushing the two circles together, thereby creating a greater area of overlap. It is fundamentally different from the win-lose approach, not only psychologically but procedurally as well.

IS THERE A BETTER WAY?

Negotiation training is underutilized in the business world and has huge potential for making people more effective in their jobs and personal lives. Unfortunately, in the past it's been approached by methods that are more antagonistic and consequently it has not become as popular as it might be. It has not been perceived by many people as personally valuable for them.

Stress training courses, for example, became popular because they were pain relieving. Negotiation training, unfortunately, is painful for many people, removes them from their comfort zones, and pushes them to be more aggressive and antagonistic, and less human than they like. Their expectation is that they will have to cope with a whole pile of adversarial techniques and bad feelings.

Many of them leave these power negotiating seminars feeling more confused about the subject than ever before, for example, "I paid all of that money for the course. I guess that means I'm going to have to put some of these hardball tactics to use just to feel like I got some value out of the class."

In addition, many negotiating training programs focus much too heavily on price-only deals, creating the impression that negotiating is nothing more than a pushing contest aimed at arriving at a final figure.

Further, the concept lacks a certain glamour as a training subject. It's been too narrowly defined in people's minds as something needed only by diplomats, politicians, labor union representatives, real estate sales people, mergers and acquisitions players, industrial buyers and their vendors, and other high-powered business people who are formally appointed to negotiate things.

Most people do not see negotiating as a personal or professional skill, useful for solving problems among departments, reducing organizational barriers, or resolving conflicts in their personal lives. The aggressive, male-oriented tactics taught in many seminars tend to offend many women, consequently, they may tend to see negotiating as primarily a male proposition.

There is hope. We have come to the point where we know enough about how to negotiate without brutalizing people, and we can make the skill of negotiating easier and less stressful to learn. The added value negotiating approach is, we feel, a true win-win method. It is a structured method for arriving at an exchange of value that satisfies the interests of all parties.

Added Value Negotiating

The objective of added value negotiating is to arrive at an agreement by *cooperatively increasing the value* involved for both parties. The process focuses on the search for balanced deals by adding value rather than extracting concessions. Each side starts by clarifying the respective interests and then searches for options that will meet them. Instead of one deal, one or both sides propose several deals.

This unique approach to negotiating:
- Offers a step-by-step method for handling any negotiating encounter, large or small.
- No positions are taken.
- Offers an up-front, honest, transparent, cards-on-the-table approach.
- Focuses on empathy in order to keep both parties within their relative comfort zones.
- Is assertive and fair.
- Eliminates one-upsmanship.
- Applies to people involved in all kinds of negotiating situations, not just buying and selling, price-only deals.

The added value negotiating method dispenses with all of those power tricks and traps in favor of a more transparent approach. Instead of the "give 'em jet lag so we can sock it to 'em" tactic, the proponent of AVN might say, "Listen, why don't we start our meeting at lunch? That will give you enough time to recover from your long plane flight and freshen up at your hotel. You won't be overly tired and you can take care of your phone calls and make any other preparations."

What does this dramatically different approach tell the other person? It suggests to him or her that you have confidence in your abilities as a negotiator. Intuitively, it tells the other person that you are fair and open. The AVN devotee will say, at least inwardly, "I don't have to try to outwit you, overpower you, or deal with you when you're tired and not thinking well. I know what my interests are and I know how I'm going to negotiate."

This is a beginning step toward building and creating empathy. How would you feel if you arrived early in the morning in a strange city and the other party said, "You must be tired. Why don't we start at noon?"

Would you interpret that gesture as a sign of weakness on his or her part? Would you see it as a gesture of confidence, empathy, and good will from somebody who wants to work out a deal?

People who say, "Oh sure, I understand the added value negotiating model and I plan to use it, but this is a dog-eat-dog world and I want to get what I need," have actually spoken in contradicting terms. If the AVN method is for you, it won't be necessary to resort to the old win-lose power traps. "But," say the doubters, "how do I keep from getting steamrolled by the other guy if he's using win-lose tactics?"

To answer this valid question, you must understand that underlying the added value negotiating philosophy is a set of human values that are the key to your success, not just as a negotiator, but as an ethical, fair human being.

You can still be human and fair while you are also assertive and interested in satisfying your own needs. These two ideas—fairness and assertiveness—are not mutually exclusive.

Frankly, if you have the mindset that you must take as much as possible and give as little as possible during any negotiating session, it will take you much longer to become comfortable with the strategies involved in added value negotiating. As you review the AVN process, you may find yourself saying, "Maybe I can get more out of the deal, rather than trying always to one-up the other person."

Maybe you'll get a better deal if the other party comes into the meeting well rested. Maybe you'll get a better deal if the other party comes into the meeting with a frame of mind that says, "We're here to cooperate."

These are all contextual elements in the negotiation that move you toward empathy and away from antipathy. One of the things you can check during any negotiation is whether you're moving closer to empathy or antipathy. Are things going smoothly? Is the relationship becoming more secure? Are you each developing rapport or is the relationship strained and full of anxiety or apprehension?

Sometimes the smallest remark, offering, or overture can turn the bad to the good. Merely suggesting you take a break and get a cup of coffee can serve to deflate building tensions and re-establish a faltering relationship. So-called power negotiators will choose these potentially deal-threatening moments to continue to hammer away at you. The AVN negotiator, by contrast, will sense problems and move to rectify them, knowing that in the end people who are more comfortable with each other will work harder together and may build a better deal for all concerned.

Before we dive fully into the concepts, descriptions, definitions, and uses of the five-stepped added value negotiating model, we need to make one thing clear. As much as we believe that the concept of added value negotiating represents a better approach to negotiating and as strongly as we feel that the principles of AVN will make you a more superior negotiator, we are not wearing rose-colored blinders about it.

After many negotiating sessions that have ranged from the simple and the direct to the complex and the antagonistic, we know the AVN method will not solve all of your negotiation problems. The approach also may not work equally well for all cases and for all people. Some people are just damned hard to negotiate with, and some deals just won't come together. Sometimes you can be as upfront and honest as possible with the other party, all to no avail. You can go out of your way to help the other party get the best deal for each of you, only to have him or her resort to power tricks or one-up tactics, without regard to your feelings or needs. That still doesn't mean you can't negotiate with them.

For your part, you don't have to play games or fall into power traps. We believe that if you're true to the AVN method, it will nearly always serve you better than would the win-lose method. For those rare cases when the other party is extremely difficult to work with and you still have some interest in making a deal, it will be no worse than the standard win-lose approach. Further, you can at least have the peace of mind of knowing that you have not sacrificed your personal values by resorting to secrecy, game-playing, aggression, bullying, or by capitulating to that kind of behavior.

While we know that because not everyone who negotiates is always kind and interested in your needs, the added value negotiating method won't work flawlessly every time, still we will make the following bold claims about the AVN method:

1. It helps you stay in your comfort zone.
2. It helps keep the other party in the comfort zone by offering choices among several feasible deals, rather than resorting to extreme offers and counteroffers.

3. It gives a whole new look to negotiating; it's not just a battle of wits in which you feel you're going to win or lose on a sudden play of the cards.

4. It helps you stay on track and know where you are in the negotiating process all of the time because it is a simple, structured method.

5. It offers an element of perceived balance where people feel both sides have value in the final deal.

6. It adds value rather than reduces it.

7. It creates better postnegotiation feelings on both sides.

AVN will help you see how more research, more planning, and more fact-finding conversations on your part will pay off in bigger, better deals that satisfy your needs and those of the other party.

Chapter Two

The Gentle Art of Added Value Negotiating

"Well, at least he's got them agreeing on something!"

WHAT MAKES A SUCCESSFUL NEGOTIATION?

Win-lose specialists consider any negotiation in which they come out ahead of the other party a success. The people who must deal with these tough, take-no-prisoners negotiators might consider any negotiation in which they survive and come out in one piece a successful one. One tries to win; the other tries not to lose.

Disguised win-lose specialists deem a successful negotiation one in which they come out on top and have the extra pleasure of knowing they outwitted the other party. It's even more fun if the other party doesn't know whether they got a good deal or not.

How about a new definition of success in negotiating? How about defining success as a situation in which both parties come away with more value than they had originally thought possible? How about a negotiation that starts out on an amicable basis and continues to develop in terms of empathy and cooperation? How about a situation in which both parties progressively discover more and more ways to add value for each other, and enhance the total value of the deal? How about a situation in which both parties are surprised and pleased to find they got some things out of the deal for which they hadn't even thought of asking?

Does this sound impossible? Well, it can be done. That's how the method of added value negotiating works.

Keep in mind, however, that not succeeding at making a deal does not always have to mean failure. Sometimes no matter how much you try and despite your best intentions, some negotiations won't work out successfully. Some just do not have success built into their circumstances. Some have too many impediments at the start, or create them as the process goes along. In other examples, the people you are dealing with for one reason or another may just not be ready to arrive at a deal. In these rare cases, either the contextual problems, difficulties with the physical environment, or personality clashes between both sides will prevent the negotiation from reaching a satisfactory conclusion.

In extreme cases, where you are trying to work with a committed win-lose player, you might decide that an acceptable deal is not in the cards, and that you don't know how to entice the person to cooperate. Sometimes you have to be willing to look the tiger in the eye and say, "It looks like we won't be able to do business together at this time," and then pack your papers and head for the door.

Added value negotiating cannot magically transform aggressive, domineering people into cooperative ones, and it can't make honest people out of dishonest ones. It can, however, influence most people to want to cooperate because it offers them a comfort level that makes aggression and game-playing less attractive than cooperation.

In any case, you know that the standard win-lose situation is the worst things can get. You may have to deal with someone who insists on doing battle, but continuing to negotiate from interests, focusing on options, and putting your cards on the table will still not put you at any greater disadvantage. In most cases, you probably won't be dealing with a hard-core win-lose person. Most people do want to negotiate cooperatively. Most do want to end up with a good deal and good feelings as well. You just have to be able to show them the way.

The objective of added value negotiating, therefore, is a process and a relationship between you and the other party that achieves the following conditions:

1. The two of you can meet and talk on a reasonably cordial, cooperative, and stress-free basis.
2. You can reach agreement fairly efficiently, without a great deal of wasted time and effort.
3. The deal you work out is balanced, that is, it has satisfactory value for both of you.
4. The two of you still have a fairly positive relationship by the time the process is complete.
5. Both of you would be willing to consider doing business together again if an opportunity were to arise.

Here's an example. A year or so ago, we concluded a very successful negotiation with a public seminar firm, involving an arrangement in which they would market a seminar based on one of our management models. What was especially interesting about the negotiation was that it involved a business venture almost exactly like one we had negotiated nearly two years previous. The objectives of the two different negotiations were so similar that they offered a very useful basis for comparing added value negotiating with the standard approach.

The previous negotiation had taken 14 months to complete and involved a great deal of antagonism between two of the parties involved with us in the deal, one a publisher and the other a coauthor. In the end, the value of the deal was fairly minimal. The seminar marketing company would pay a royalty for each seminar it sold. The royalty would be divided among the three parties involved. By the time the deal was signed, two of the parties were no longer on speaking terms, and the executives of the marketing company felt very uncomfortable about the whole enterprise.

The negotiation had followed the standard course of offer, counteroffer, counteroffer, ad nauseum. Each round of offer and counteroffer was punctuated by an exchange of angry letters and accusations. For our part, we had simply taken a flexible stance early in the process and stood back while the others fought. By the end, most of the players were sorry it had even happened. They had a deal, but not a very good one; nobody was happy.

In contrast, the second negotiation, with different players involved, followed the AVN method. We explained the method to the executives of the seminar firm and asked if they would be willing to try it. They were, especially when we explained that the previous negotiation had taken 14 months to complete.

We concluded the deal in six weeks, from the time of the first telephone conversation to a signed agreement. The deal involved considerably more value for us and for them and included options for marketing the seminars internationally as well as in the United States, cooperative sales of books and audiotapes based on the subject matter, and an agreement on in-house marketing of the seminars as well as public presentations.

The second deal involved no shouting, no angry letters or faxes, no accusations, and no ruptured relationships. Why? This is primarily because the leaders of the seminar firm watched the value of their side of the deal progressively grow and develop, instead of watching it shrink under the onslaughts of counter-proposals. They were fascinated to see the business possibilities blossom as we worked our way systematically through the method.

After years of using the AVN method, we have had some experiences in which we couldn't seem to get anywhere with the other party. We've had far more in which the other party was quite taken with the benefits of the method and were often even bemused by its simplicity and openness, though. It works.

ARM-TWISTING: WHEN IS A NEGOTIATION NOT A NEGOTIATION?

Just to clarify a small but very significant point: A negotiation is not a negotiation when one of the parties involved is powerless, either politically or psychologically, to say no to the other. If you find yourself in such a predicament, you must face the reality of the situation and deal with it as it is. If you don't have no-power, it isn't a negotiation. If the situation is so over-balanced in favor of the other side that you desperately need them and they don't need you very much, then you basically have to do whatever they say. The techniques we're dealing with in this book aren't designed for those situations.

At the close of the first major military action of the Persian Gulf War in January 1991, representatives from the Iraqi army met with American General H. Norman Schwarzkopf, leader of the United Nations allied forces, to discuss the terms of a cease-fire. When quizzed by reporters on the way to the meeting, Schwarzkopf remarked, "This is not a negotiation. We're going there to dictate the terms of a surrender. They will accept the terms we specify or else the fighting will continue."

Iraq's military machine had been virtually demolished, its economy was in shambles, and tens of thousands of its supposedly elite forces had turned into unarmed and starving refugees. The devastation of the allied bombing, coupled with a decisive military thrust into Kuwait, had crippled Iraq's ability to fight. The meeting between the Iraqis and Schwarzkopf was, indeed, not a negotiation.

A number of people, on first exposure to added value negotiating, ask questions like "What do I do in a situation where I'll go out of business unless I can sell my product to the one big distributor in the industry?" "What if I need my wife (husband, girl friend, boy friend) so desperately that I'm willing to do anything to get her (him) back?" and "What if my home is at the point of foreclosure, or my business is at the door of bankruptcy, and someone is offering me a pittance for it?"

These questions all more or less contain their own answers, don't they? If self-destruction is not an acceptable option, then you do whatever the person wielding the whip says. You're in an unfortunate situation, but it isn't a negotiation.

Some situations that may look like negotiations at the outset may actually turn out to be situations in which there really is no negotiating to do. You might come to the realization that you need them and they really don't need you very much. In other cases, a seemingly hopeless situation may turn into a negotiation when the underdog discovers, or realizes, he or she already possesses something the other side needs and is not in a position to get by coercion.

For example, the supposed top dog in the situation may have a greater need to do business with the underdog than might be obvious at first. A popular plot concept in movies has the carnivorous corporation thwarted in its efforts to roll over the small company, small town, or mom-and-pop business because the underdog holds some kind of trump card.

Recently inventor Robert W. Kearns found that Chrysler Corporation had used his design for an intermittent windshield wiper system in its cars without paying him for it. Although the situation first seemed like a very small David facing a very large Goliath, nevertheless he negotiated a $17 million deal with Chrysler for the rights to use his design. He probably could have won more in a lawsuit, but in view of his age and the attractiveness of that amount of money, both he and Chrysler found it in their best interests to negotiate rather than to undergo a very long and costly litigation.

It's always a good idea to think about any situation carefully before you decide that negotiation is not possible. In such a situation, there's no point in abusing yourself for not getting a better deal when in fact there is really no deal in the cards.

The technique of added value negotiating will, however, enable you to take careful inventory of the elements of value you have at your disposal for offer to the other party and to make the most of their potential.

LET'S DEFINE OUR TERMS

To develop a method for added value negotiating, let's clarify the terminology involved. Let's define some of the critical terms we'll be using, and see how a more precise language can help you think more clearly and communicate more effectively. Here are some proposed definitions of the key terms. Because we're basically talking about building deals, let's begin with a definition of a deal.

Deal—an exchange of value between two (or more) parties that satisfies their respective interests.

Value—the substance or medium of exchange in a negotiation; various tangible and intangible elements which can be traded off for one another as a way of satisfying the respective interests.

Interests—the unique needs, desires, aspirations, or outcomes which the parties in a negotiation seek to satisfy.

Negotiation—a process for arriving at an exchange of value that satisfies the interests of all parties involved.

Options—various ways of packaging the elements of value involved in a negotiation. Options are *not* the same as interests; they are ways to *satisfy* interests.

Notice that we define negotiation in terms of the three prior concepts, i.e., deal, value, and interests. The emphasis here is on the *exchange of value* rather than on your own individual gains from the deal. This exchange of value must *meet interests* for it to result in a successful deal. Note that added value negotiating is a *process* or a method. It is something you do and a way of doing it.

Please review these definitions several times and keep them in mind through the remainder of this book. These five key definitions—deal, value, interests, negotiation, and options—are almost all we need to develop a radically different approach to making an agreement.

ADDED VALUE NEGOTIATING: THE PHILOSOPHY AND THE PROCESS

The Philosophy

As previously emphasized, much of the psychology and the metaphorical symbology that surrounds negotiating emphasizes an antagonistic relationship. We picture people sitting on opposite sides of a bargaining table. They come to the meeting as opposing delegations, sometimes closely observed by journalists and other onlookers. They come bearing proposals that they intend to offer. The smoke-filled room is an ancient metaphor for the context of labor negotiations.

This us-versus-them visual picture does plenty to reinforce the two-camps mentality that dominates the negotiation and gives it the I win–you lose flavor.

Early in the research and experimentation with the AVN model, it became clear that if it were possible to more or less turn over the negotiation to some kind of a structured process and to have the process guide the search for value, it might be possible to depersonalize the problems involved. It might be a way to eliminate or reduce the adversarial tone of the relationship by putting the focus on the ingredients of the deal rather than on the actions and counteractions of the players involved. This led to the concentration on added value negotiating as a distinct method, or process, in contrast to a winning-by-your-wits skill.

This radical shift is, for many people, a blessing of great importance. Many people tend to view negotiating as a psychologically risky experience because of the back-and-forth pushing and pulling they anticipate. They tend to have an unconscious or intuitive fear that they might suddenly lose out because they weren't quick enough to fend off the other side's demands, or because they were pressured to agree too quickly to something. A negotiating process that did not depend on personal aggressiveness, quick thinking, or having inside information about the other party would, it seems, be very appealing to many people.

With AVN, the joint search for value in the deal puts each party side by side at the negotiating table, rather than across from each other. This visual imagery shows AVN as an approach that encourages harmony and cooperation. Both sides win when someone comes up with an acceptable deal that meets everyone's needs.

Added value negotiating is an impersonal negotiating approach, although decidedly not an inhuman one. The process is less confrontational and focuses not on emotions and arguments, but rather on getting more value in the deal for both sides. To this extent the method has a paradoxical quality. One of the hardest things for win-lose fans to grasp is that the more you give, the more you can get. The more you give of yourself in terms of options, ideas, suggestions, and help to the other party, the better you will probably do in the final deal.

Of course this doesn't always happen, but in the majority of negotiating situations, if you try to help the other side to see what you want and to help them figure out what exactly they want, much of the game playing and warfare disappears. When two people spend their time mutually looking for ways they can make a deal, the negotiation takes on a joint-venture quality.

The Process

Just as the philosophy of added value negotiating is deceptively simple, so too is the process. Indeed, it is simplicity itself.

First, you take the trouble to understand as completely as possible the interests of the other party with respect to the matter under consideration. What need, problem, or issue do they seek to fulfill, solve, or resolve? What is it that brings them to consider making some sort of deal with you?

Next, you take inventory of the various elements of value that could possibly be involved in an arrangement between you. What do you have that they might want? What do they have that you might want? In what ways could joint action possibly serve the interests of both?

The next step in AVN is the one that sets it apart from all other major negotiating methods we have studied. While virtually all methods have one party approaching the other with a proposal, AVN offers the other party a range of alternatives to choose from. This is such a critical element in its success that it is one of the few definite rules:

Never make just one offer.
Always present several alternatives.

The powerful psychological benefit of this aspect of the method will become clear as we go along. We will explore ways to create attractive alternatives to offer.

Once you and the other party have arrived at several, not just one, possible arrangements of value, i.e., alternative *deal packages,* then there ensues a cooperative examination of these deal packages against the interests of both parties. If there exist one or more deal packages both you and the other party can say yes to, then you're almost home. If not, you can simply design some more variations and evaluate those. If you have thoroughly identified the various elements of value available to the parties in the deal and subdivided them into their logical variations, you will usually discover that it is possible to create literally thousands of combinations. It takes only one good combination to have a successful deal.

The real trick to working with the alternative deal packages is to make them reasonably balanced at the outset, so both parties will feel fairly comfortable with the possibilities they represent.

Here is the second critical point of difference with added value negotiating: It avoids offers and counteroffers by focusing on a mutually beneficial search for value. Most negotiating methods portray one party as offering half a loaf and the other party as demanding two loaves, with both hoping to settle in the neighborhood of one loaf. The AVN approach, on the other hand, starts with a loaf of bread, plus butter and some jam. As the two parties work together, they figure out how to toast the bread as well, and maybe even add some peanut butter.

This brings up the second firm rule of added value negotiating:

Put the value up front.
Don't work by demanding and extracting concessions.

It is here, working with these two precepts, that the AVN model takes a sharp turn and leaves the conventional road of negotiating. The combination of the multiple-option approach and the balanced-deal approach puts the negotiation on a completely different psychological ground from the familiar win-lose context. Tough negotiators are appalled at first by the apparent innocence and naivete of this method. "You must be crazy," they say. "You *never* make your best offer at the start. You've trapped yourself; you have no room to make concessions." Let's explore how this supposedly naive approach works.

Concessions are outlawed in AVN, just as offers and counteroffers are outlawed. They are part of the combative, scarcity-driven mentality of win-lose. The AVN method accomplishes the objective by a completely different psychological route. What happens, for instance, when you sit down with the other party after clearly defining the interests on both sides and taking stock of the elements of value involved, and both of you design several interestingly different deal packages? Suppose you formulate two or three and they formulate two or three others, subject to the proviso that each must offer a semblance of balanced value for both parties?

At this point, you have deprived both negotiators of their enemies. Neither has an opponent or an opposer as one writer calls it. Each is in the position of merely saying yes or no to a choice of deal packages with the understanding that a no is perfectly acceptable. The trick, if there is one, becomes a matter of coming up with balanced combinations of value, not offers that the other side is forced to counter.

Once the parties involved have identified at least one feasible deal package to which both can say yes, the process becomes one of refining, adding value, and perfecting the deal.

We will have much more to say about the specific methods and tools of added value negotiating as we continue. The most important point here is that it is possible to construct an altogether different psychological context for the negotiation and to eliminate most of the adversarial tone of the process. By working through the AVN process and trusting its principles, you can often accomplish things not possible with the standard win-lose methods.

KEY INGREDIENT #1: EMPATHY

Empathy between the negotiating parties is a powerful ingredient for the success of the negotiation. What do we mean by empathy? In the context of any interaction between human beings, empathy is a feeling of affinity, the inclination to move with and toward the other person. The opposite of empathy is antipathy, a sense of alienation and an inclination to move against and away from the other person.

While it's not necessary for negotiators to fall in love with one another, some degree of warmth, affability, and trust will go a long way toward improving the contextual environment of the negotiation. It is this psychological environment that the AVN method seeks to create and to use to the best advantage for the parties involved. You need to consciously check to see where you are on the empathy-antipathy scale as you go along in the negotiation. It will give you a better idea about how to manage your side of the process.

If you have a strong sense of empathy with the other party, you can begin to direct more of your energy toward the mechanics of a good deal, rather than dealing with emotional issues, hostility, and personality clashes.

Empathy can operate both as cause and effect in a negotiation. When things are going well and people are discovering that the basis for their cooperation is becoming broader and more valuable, good feelings naturally result. Conversely, when one or more parties have the social awareness and interpersonal skills to build and maintain a climate of openness and cooperation, the empathy thus created supports their mutual search for value. They become more willing to look for ways to add value and more generous in their spirit of cooperation.

As negotiators, Americans sometimes tend to neglect the psychological context of the process, in favor of the mechanics, and especially in favor of money issues. People from other cultural backgrounds can sometimes find themselves very ill at ease with the "get to the point" approach. They may be accustomed to setting up the psychological context with various social preliminaries such as get-to-know-you meetings over tea, coffee, a drink, or a meal. They may have different orientations to factors such as time, nonverbal messages of affinity, ways of signaling status and authority, and symbolic gestures that convey cooperation. Sensitivity to the social context and to the differing social values and styles of others can often be a critical asset in negotiating.

Throughout any negotiation, you must continuously assess the level of empathy between yourself and the other negotiating party. If it's low and there is a growing sense of discomfort or even outright hostility, your negotiation will probably not succeed as you would like. If it's high, then both parties will tend to go deeper, searching for mutual elements of value and looking for more ways to make an already good deal better.

If any one negotiating session starts moving in the direction of antipathy, maybe you need to go back to the earlier stages and reestablish the relationship by reaffirming the need for trust, honesty, and cooperation in the deal. Remember, it's not just numbers, dollars, yen, marks, or pounds; eggs and butter; tons of coal; and bushels of wheat. It's people and their positive feelings about you and about themselves that can make the deal good for all involved.

KEY INGREDIENT #2: FOCUSING ON INTERESTS

If empathy is the heart or the emotional-interpersonal part of the AVN approach, then surely the mental part is its intensive focus on interests. The concept of negotiating from interests can lend clarity and logic to what might otherwise be a confused process of give and take.

In the context of the AVN philosophy, values, and methods, it is remarkable how poorly conceived most negotiating processes are. It is common practice for one party to start with a list of must-have elements of value, throw in some extra demands to provide slack for concessions, and simply go to the other party with an unbalanced offer in hopes of ending up with the most wanted elements. Often, the preparation process gets no more attention than this. The person who initiates the process with the first offer may set his or her sights high, but at the same time will probably set them too narrow.

The offer-counteroffer approach typically focuses on a few key elements of value, usually revolving around some form of money proposition. Relatively few people think broadly about the subject of the negotiation in order to discover additional areas of possible value beyond the obvious and accepted ones.

This is what a focus on interests does for you. It opens up new areas of possible value that may not be obvious at first thought. When you get clear in your own mind what your interests are in a certain proposition, you open up your wide-angle lens to consider more potential elements of value. When you understand the interests of your counterpart, your mind automatically starts working in terms of things or actions that can appeal to those interests. When you can offer value that appeals to the other party's interests, you can then expect to receive balancing value that serves your own interests.

In addition, a focus on interests is the start of a shift in emphasis from people and personalities to value and benefits. It helps to de-personalize the process and eliminate much of the apprehension. This is why it could be called *structured negotiating* as readily as added value negotiating. There is a method and a comfortable structure that take much of the uncertainty and ambiguity out of the negotiating process.

There is another important feature of a focus on interests. Interests are, for the most part, indisputable. Your interests are whatever you deem them to be. If you approach the other party with a demand of some sort, you can expect to have to justify that demand in some way. When you explain your interests, no one has a right to dispute them; they are aspects of your personal construction of reality. The other party may question whether you are being realistic, or even being honest, but in the end you are the arbiter of your interests.

When people begin to realize that in declaring their interests they are taking the power that is due them in connection with their roles as negotiators, they usually begin to feel more confident and more empowered in the situation. They have the right to decide what does and doesn't serve their interests. In added value negotiating, you always have the power to say no. Your veto is the ultimate expression of the fact that you are in charge of your side of the situation.

KEY INGREDIENT #3: WORKING FROM OPTIONS

A third key ingredient of the AVN method is the process of developing options rather than hoping to push the other party into going along with an offer you have made. This gives you a sense of power in your ability to conjure up various deal packages with various different appeals. It gives the other party a sense of power because there is no obligation to accept a single offer and no compulsion to counterattack with another offer. It also gives everyone involved a wider comfort zone because options are easier to work with than take-it-or-leave-it offers.

When you start systematically identifying and analyzing the various elements of value in a typical negotiating situation, you will often find a wealth of possibilities available for constructing deals. Make a habit of thinking about virtually every aspect of a deal in terms of options. Is there money involved? Try to work out a range of different prices or payments, each one a tradeoff against one or more other elements of value. How about variations in the schedule of payments: all at once, a series of payments, payment in material as well as money, and so on. What about rights? All related rights or selected rights? One-nation rights or world rights? For what various possible periods of time?

Many people who begin to gain a bit of experience with the AVN method find themselves wondering how they could have ever been so crude in past negotiating situations as to come up with only one offer and that a poorly constructed offer in terms of overall value. They begin to realize that even with a relatively small range of options for a few major elements of value, there are many possible combinations available. Why limit one's thinking to only one particular construction of value, which is typically only an opening gambit anyway? Why not think through the various possibilities for deals and come up with an assortment of choices that have different kinds of appeals?

This is also the point at which the AVN method makes the negotiator feel more confident. When you realize that you can put together literally hundreds or even thousands of different deal packages for the other side to consider, and you can make all of them balanced well enough to meet your needs, then you understand that negotiating need not be a game or a contest. It becomes an intelligent, well-organized, and dispassionate process of identifying value and designing ways to make it real.

THE FIVE-STEP ADDED VALUE
NEGOTIATING METHOD

One of the most encouraging things about a five-step negotiating method is that there are only five steps. This makes the AVN approach easier to remember in situations that get complicated or involve the interests of a number of parties.

The steps follow a logical order, taking the negotiation from the big picture, where you and the other party gather information about your needs, down to the more concrete, as you prepare, analyze, and choose from a number of deal packages. The five simple steps are as follows:

1. **Clarify interests.**
2. **Identify options.**

3. **Design deal packages.**
4. **Select the best deal.**
5. **Perfect the deal.**

Communication between the two parties is a critical key to your success with the method. The more you and the other person talk about the issues on the table, the better chance you have of coming up with deals that meet both of your needs. Even if the other person plays it close to the chest and does not divulge very much information, the AVN method is flexible enough to allow you to make certain assumptions about what he or she may need. While it's certainly easier to negotiate with people who tell you what they want, by following the method closely and drawing some conclusions based on the information you gather or interpret, you can put together a number of deals for the other party to choose.

Let's review the five-step method in more detail.

Step 1: Clarify Interests

Before you can even begin to formulate some possible deals, you must know what you want and what the other party wants out of the negotiation. The AVN method starts with a search for interests on both sides.

Let's separate the interests into two distinct categories: subjective interests and objective interests.

Subjective interests are judgmental. They relate to interests that are intangible, personal, and perception-based. Examples of some subjective interests might be the concept of goodwill in business, a longterm relationship with the other party, or the chance to enter a particular market.

Objective interests are measurable. They relate to interests that are tangible, observable, and recognizable. Whereas subjective interests are more abstract, that is, you can't really see them or hold them in your hand, objective interests are much more concrete. Examples of some objective interests are cash, the deed to a building, or the use of a computer.

The window of interest.   One of the easiest ways to classify the interests involved—both subjective and objective—is to use a pen-and-paper four-square model called the window of interest, as shown in Figure 2–1.

FIGURE 2–1
The Window of Interest

	We want:	They want:
Subjective interests (judgmental)	• Intangible • Personal • Perception-based	
Objective interests (measurable)	• Tangible • Observable • Recognizable	

The window of interest is a figurative window made up of what you want in one column and what the other party wants in the other. You can categorize your respective subjective and objective interests, making a list of each and capturing the interests on paper for later review.

The benefit of this simple model is that it not only clarifies interests for both of you in a physically readable form, but it also helps to point out mutual interests you both may have. Seeing them on paper can trigger a mutual response to your common goals. The window of interest can get the negotiation process moving quickly because it gets both parties talking and documenting their interests on paper. Because one or both parties can create the window of interest model, it gets the ball rolling and places the emphasis of this early stage of the negotiation on productivity rather than posturing, overblown emotional issues, or long harangues.

For example, if you own an office building and are negotiating with a potential tenant, one of the interests you both may share is the desire for a long-term relationship. You want to keep a rent-paying tenant for several years and the tenant may want to sign a long lease that locks him or her into the same rental figure. While you may not agree on everything at first, this desire to establish a long-term business relationship can indicate at least one area of mutual interest for you both.

Step 2: Identify Options

Every negotiation involves a number of elements of value. Depending upon the complexity of the deal being sought, these may range from a short few to several hundred. As you finish the window of interest and move on in the negotiation, take stock of the elements of value available in the deal. Ask yourself the following questions:

1. What are the elements of value in the deal, both tangible and intangible?
2. What can I give that they need?
3. What can they give me that I need?
4. How can we both add value to the deal?

For the purposes of the AVN method, you can divide the elements of value into five separate categories. As you review any deal, keep these elements in mind and ask yourself some questions about each one:

1. *Money.* How much money is involved? How will it be paid? Under what conditions? When? Where?
2. *Property.* Is it intangible or tangible? How much property? All of it or portions of it? Where is it?
3. *Actions.* What will you agree to do (or refrain from doing) for the other party? What will the other party agree to do (or refrain from doing) for you?
4. *Rights.* What rights can they give you? What rights can you give them?
5. *Risks.* What risks are apparent in the deal? What risks are hidden? What risks could you take? What risks could the other party take?

The option tree.   Just as the first step of the AVN method uses a pen-and-paper model, the second step calls for you to design an option tree as a way of keeping physical track of the various elements of value, as Figure 2–2 demonstrates. How you use the option tree depends on your own organizing style.

The option tree, like the window of interest, helps you and the other party to identify similar elements of value right away. If time is short, highlight the shared elements of value and focus on them to help you start formulating some potential deal. If time is more on your side, go back over each of the five elements and look deeper for what you can provide

FIGURE 2–2
The Option Tree

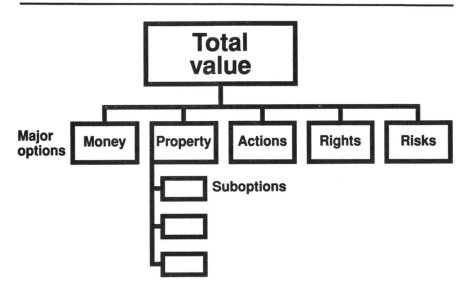

or what the other party can provide. Sometimes you can make suggestions about what they might be able to do for you and vice versa.

Once you've established the elements of value, you can now move on to the third step of the added value negotiating method, where you become a bit more focused on the actual deals.

Step 3: Design Deal Packages

What makes AVN so different from most other negotiating methods is its use of multiple deals. Instead of creating one offer and trying to force it onto the other party—à la win-lose—you design several possible deals, two, three, five, or even seven. Using a Chinese-menu approach (pick something from this column and something from that column, etc.), you can scan the window of interest and the option tree and create a series of deals, each with its own special appeal.

Here are some additional steps to consider as you design some deals:

1. Design the deals so that each one includes options in each of the five elements of value.
2. Never make just one offer; always create a group of deals.

3. Design deal packages—various combinations of the value elements that seem to balance the interests of all parties.
4. Verify that each deal offers a different way to balance interests, through a different arrangement of the value elements.

Using the sale of your house as an example, you could focus one deal on getting the most amount of money possible. Another deal could focus not so much on the sales price, but on how the money will be paid, who will carry the note, and so forth. Another deal could allow you to have a long escrow so you can stay in town longer, and still another deal could make the sale of your house contingent on the sale of the other party's home. You could arrange to leave all of your furniture in one deal, swap houses with the buyer in another, or have the house repainted, recarpeted, and recurtained.

Each deal may be balanced but significantly different in its design. The beauty of added value negotiating is that with so many deals to choose from, you and the other party are very likely to find at least one that meets all of your needs.

The deal creation process can last several minutes or several weeks, again depending upon the complexity of the subject at hand and your time deadlines. You may be able to complete the entire AVN process in one meeting or it may take months to reach an agreement. By following the steps in the process, you can make sure you don't leave out any of the things that are important to you. By discussing everything with the other party, you may even come across interests, elements of value, or creative deals you didn't even realize.

Step 4: Select the Best Deal

Once you've created at least two or three deals, it's time to get a bit more critical of them and analyze them carefully. If you designed each deal on your own, taking the other party's needs into consideration, you'll need to give him or her time to evaluate what you have put together.

You may need to go through your own period of inspection and review, looking at each deal from your own perspective. As you analyze each deal, look at it in terms of the following criteria:

1. *Value*. How much value does the deal incorporate? For each party? In total?

2. *Balance.* Does the deal offer equal or comparable value for all parties?
3. *Overall approach.* Do all elements of the deal go together into an effective solution to all interests?
4. *Appeal.* Is there at least one deal to which all parties can say "yes" to?

If the answer to the last question is "no," then you need to go back to AVN Step 3 (design deal packages) and take a harder look at the window of interest, the option tree, and the type and scope of the deals you designed. Maybe there are just one or two pieces of critical information that you need to know to fill in the puzzle for you. Maybe the other party has neglected to tell you the one thing that will turn the entire negotiation around. Maybe you each need to do a bit more research about some subject.

Once you've evaluated each of the deals on the merits, and you agree that there is at least one acceptable deal of the group, it's time to select one and then move to the fifth step of the AVN method.

All it takes for a negotiation to be successful is the existence of at least one deal package to which all parties can say "yes." Let's say that you've created four total deals. The other party likes Deal 2 and 4, but not the other two. You prefer Deal 2. By process of elimination, you can now focus your energies on Deal 2.

By giving a wider choice of deals, you make the other party feel like he or she has more of a say in the negotiation, more of a vested interest in the outcome than if you just proposed one deal and tried to force it on him or her.

To get closure on a deal, follow these steps:

1. Narrow the evaluation to feasible deals, i.e., deals that appeal to all parties. There is no point in discussing deals that neither party likes.
2. If there are no feasible deals, go back to Step 3 and create more for discussion and consideration.
3. Compare all feasible deals (if more than one) and settle on one you both like best.

Step 5: Perfect the Deal

There is a tendency for people to want to rush things as they reach this stage of the process. There is more involved at this point than just dotting the *i*'s and crossing the *t*'s. This is your opportunity to make sure you've covered all of the important details, that the relationship is still healthy, and that you have a written agreement with which all parties can live.

It's important to refine the selected deal, make sure it's balanced in terms of total value, and ensure that all the parties are comfortable with it. Once you've chosen the deal that works best, you can tighten up various particulars, perhaps add extra items of value, and iron out the details together. Many people find, to their great relief, that getting through all five steps of the added value negotiating method is not difficult or stressful, especially compared to the typical tug-of-war they must do during a win-lose negotiating encounter.

Later, we will explore the value of plain-English agreements as ways to build trust and strengthen the deal, as we work with the techniques of the fifth stage in more depth.

These five steps are the basic marching plan of added value negotiating. By thinking through each step carefully, by doing your homework properly during each step, you have the best chance to maintain empathy, build a solid relationship with the other party, and make sure both of you get superior value from the deal.

THE MEET-AND-CONFER CYCLE

Not everything in life is a one-meeting, one-shot deal. Barring the occasional see-it-and-buy-it approach that works well when purchasing certain products and services, most high-ticket or high-importance deals take time to develop, analyze, and research. This is why we need a systematic approach to communicating during the negotiation process.

Americans tend to like their deals like their hamburgers, put together and ready to grab and consume. Unlike the Japanese, for example, who tend to prefer to study each facet of any deal, almost to the point of minutiae, Yanks want to hear the other party's pitch, make their own, and then settle on one of them.

The phrase *it's a done deal* is characteristic to the American culture. While this fastbreak approach works well in some cases, especially those involving small matters, tight time deadlines, or no chain of command in the decision-making process, it can only make things worse during large-scale negotiations.

Some of your deals will require you to prepare a tremendous amount of material and do plenty of research before you even meet with the other party. Other episodes will require you to do further study after you and the other party have designed various deals. Still other negotiations may take place over time spans as short as a few days or as long as several years. During these breaks, when you're not actually "at the table," you'll be evaluating your interests in comparison with the other party's.

The meet-and-confer cycle is a way to do exactly that—meet with the other party and clarify various issues as the negotiation continues. It may take one meeting or one dozen, depending on the complexity of your subject and the needs of you and the other person.

Prior to or after a series of meetings with the other party, you may need to have conversations with other people in your group, do more research, establish new criteria, make phone calls, read reports, or conduct any other preparatory movements to help you understand what you're going to do.

To use the meet-and-confer cycle effectively, keep these things in mind:

1. Don't be in a hurry to get things over with—take as much time as you need, within reason and courtesy to the other party, to clarify your interests and answer any questions you may have encountered between sessions.

2. Work from knowledge, insight, and research. Your desire to build your relationship with the other person, gather information that will help the negotiation, and understand the situation is more important than making bunches of proposals.

3. If you need more time, take it. It's more important to be right than try to wing it and stab blindly in the dark, especially for highly critical issues.

There can be a number of negative consequences if you don't understand the other side well. If you go to the other side with a proposal and you really haven't explored what their views, values, or purposes really are, what problems they have, or what issues they need to clear up, you can leave yourself at their mercy.

Without knowing what they want, or worse, not knowing what you want, you may force yourself into a position where you make an ill-prepared offer to someone who is less than charitable to you. This person can then counterattack your one offer, especially if he or she comes from the old I win–you lose school of negotiating. His or her hidden agenda or desire to get the upper hand can sabotage the negotiation before it even begins.

To use the meet-and-confer cycle effectively, follow the AVN method. After your initial encounter with the other person, meet again to clarify the issues on both sides. You may even want to send a letter or a memo that says, "Here's my understanding of what we discussed last week. We agreed that we both have the following interests. . . ."

Consistently make sure you and the other party are on the right track together. Your subsequent meetings can help each of you to pinpoint the value involved in your deal and how to best meet each other's needs.

The number of times you go through the meet-and-confer cycle depends upon the complexity of the negotiation, the time deadlines each of you face, and the practicality of the meeting locations, times, and schedules. You could do it all in one session or in a number of them. While it's always preferable to meet face-to-face to maintain the requirements of good human interaction, telephone meetings will suffice if time and travel distance make in-person meetings prohibitive. In a high-tech environment, you might even do some of it by electronic mail.

During the early stages of the meet-and-confer cycle, you only want to talk about options and ways of dividing the different elements of value. You aren't talking about specific deals yet, just the different interests and options related to the negotiation itself.

Look at this stage of the negotiation as a refining process. You are trying to go from the big picture down to the smaller one, boiling the entire negotiation process down from dozens or even hundreds of different elements of value to a more manageable number.

The next time you meet, you and the other party can then start to explore or even create various deal packages.

After you've begun to work on deal packages, you still have the option to step back and say, "We need some more refinement," "We need to see if any of these deals would really work," etc. If so, meet again after you've examined the possibilities.

THE ATTITUDE, SPIRIT, AND GOALS OF ADDED VALUE NEGOTIATING

The attitude of AVN followers is breathtakingly simple: "We're looking for a good deal and we're perfectly happy to give you a good deal so that we will get a good deal in return. We're willing to negotiate openly and honestly, but we won't be taken for a ride either. We have certain interests in mind, and we're assuming you have some too. We will try to determine what those interests are and how certain options can meet those interests.

"We plan to tell you what interests we have and we hope you'll tell us too. If we have mutual interests, so much the better. If you don't tell us what your interests are, we will make certain assumptions based on what we know already and what we can guess. We'll create a group of deal packages based upon our interests and the options that suit them. We'll know what works best for us and we'll try to establish what group of deals may work best for you. We reserve the right to use our veto power if we feel the negotiation is deteriorating into a strict win-lose pushing and shoving contest. These are the rules by which we plan to operate for this negotiation."

The spirit of AVN is based on openness, flexibility, and the mutual search for the successful exchange of value. You try to build strong relationships with people over time. The main goal of added value negotiating comes down to one thing: better deals than could be achieved by any other method.

Other secondary goals include building long-term business connections, lasting relationships, and acceptance from the other party. If you have the reputation of being a fair and honest negotiator, better deals will come your way. If your reputation brings to mind the typical I win–you lose operator, some people will go out of their way to avoid you.

Recall our book-writing colleague from the first chapter. He may get the best deal for him from the publisher at that time, but it's always a one-shot never-again deal for them. By contrast, the added value negotiating proponent would see the author-publisher arrangement as a potentially lucrative, long-term relationship and seek to add value to any deal.

YOUR PERSONAL VALUES, PEOPLE SKILLS, AND COMFORT ZONES

Much of negotiating is portrayed as something that is only for business. You'll find virtually every known negotiating book is in the business section in the bookstore or library. Articles about the subject appear in the business trade journals and newspapers, and training seminars are geared for and marketed to business people. While it's certainly true that business people are the most likely candidates for the subject, it's also fair to say negotiating has other more personal applications. In addition to straight business deals, try using the AVN model for personal issues (e.g., family or other interpersonal conflict resolutions, sibling differences, marriage negotiations) and other social context encounters.

The power of the AVN method is that when you feel threatened, uncomfortable, or apprehensive about how the negotiation is proceeding, you just simply buckle down a bit harder and continue to focus on the process itself. By following the steps in order and letting the various information areas fill in you can negotiate with even the powermonger with more confidence in yourself.

There tends to be a greater sense of confidence, control, and even relief when you can tell the other side, "Let's use this negotiating method I know. It may help us figure out what we want and what we can do to meet our needs."

Once you feel comfortable with the AVN process, it takes the focus off the interpersonal attacks and the battle of wits that interfere with many negotiating sessions and places it upon the methodical search for joint value.

Some people find that the AVN method fits well with their personality style and approach to business and personal encounters that involve negotiating. Others who may have more adversarial habits may be a bit confused about the AVN approach initially. To some the AVN approach may even appear wishy-washy or weak. Once you know what the AVN approach stresses in terms of meeting your own self-interests, you'll find it is more effective than the standard win-lose approach at getting what you want and without all of the attached tactical warfare baggage.

Throughout this book, we will operate on the assumption that the majority of people are not so-called professional negotiators, highly trained in the tough and powerful school of negotiation; that they are somewhat out of their comfort zone when they have to negotiate a difficult or complicated issue; and that they are basically interested in getting a good deal for themselves without actively seeking to harm the other party.

It's from this framework that the idea of personal values becomes such an important part of the AVN process. If you take great pride in one-upping the other party, if you get an ego-inflating kick out of hammering the best deal possible out of your opponent, or if you go to great lengths to make sure the other person knows you won and he or she lost, then this is probably not the best method for you.

People who have a marked tendency to emotionalize or personalize every issue, especially seemingly trivial ones, will also have more trouble negotiating with the AVN method than those who don't. One of your main concerns about using the approach should be to stay within your own comfort zone and to allow and even to help the other person to stay within his or hers. Human stress levels can really skyrocket when we find ourselves out of our element, even for a relatively short time. If you try to initiate tricks and tactics that make the other person uncomfortable, things can come to a grinding halt as he or she tries to regroup and get back into the comfort zone.

If your personal values tend toward humanity, empathy, and honesty to begin with, you'll probably find the AVN approach will work well for you. If you are equipped to cope with personality conflicts, can discern information, and can put another person at ease, your proficiency as an AVN negotiator will know few limits.

Added value negotiating as an approach seeks to capitalize on our better qualities: openness, honesty, transparency, and a sense of negotiating from the standpoint of the greater good for all concerned. Added value negotiating is not and never will be an I'll-get-you approach to negotiating. It seeks to find the best deals for all concerned by clarifying each other's interests, identifying options to meet those interests, and creating, evaluating, and choosing from a number of deal packages that make both parties happy.

By patiently following the steps of the approach, you can effectively deal with the tough negotiators just as you would the more passive ones. The approach works whether the other person gives you a lot of information or very little, plenty of help or a small amount. If you're dealing with a tight-lipped person, you'll certainly have to work a bit harder and make some assumptions about his or her options and interests, but that should not daunt you from being creative yourself and using the approach to help you work out the best deal.

People are often as surprisingly similar as they are different. By modeling the behaviors taught in the AVN approach—openness, empathy, honesty, transparency, and working for the greater good—you can often persuade the tough negotiators and the introverts to follow the process.

Chapter Three

The Bulldog, the Fox, and the Deer
Negotiating Styles

*"God bless the old gentleman.
He simply <u>thrives</u> on controversy."*

EACH PERSON NEGOTIATES IN HIS OR HER OWN WAY

How people approach a negotiating experience depends heavily on their individual personalities, psychological makeup, self-esteem, long-held views and values about themselves and others, and their deeply-rooted personal hypotheses about what it takes to succeed in the world. Each of us has a characteristic style as a negotiator. If you understand the way a person tends to approach a negotiation, you needn't waste time and energy trying to influence him or her in unsuccessful ways.

A negotiating encounter is also colored by all the past experiences each person has had. Each person has usually formed some general idea about how to approach a negotiating situation to get something. It's not unlike any other new experience based on past history. If you were bitten by a big dog early in life, chances are high that big dogs give you a queasy feeling when you meet them.

Similarly, if a person's indoctrination into negotiating was flavored by a bad experience, that is, a power negotiator who ran roughshod over them, then that person might feel at least a bit uncomfortable each time it's necessary to negotiate something important. They have no precedent for thinking that the engagement will be friendly, value-oriented, positive, or easy. These preconceived notions can force an otherwise normal and friendly person to act in a number of strange and negative ways, ranging from a hardnosed aggressor to a crafty tactician or a shy avoider.

None of these responses may reflect their true personalities, but because they serve as effective defense mechanisms against those big, bad, professional negotiators they've met in other encounters, they choose to try to put on new personas.

One of the first things you'll need to do as an added value negotiator is to learn to identify and understand the various behavior patterns of your negotiating counterparts. If you have an accurate sense of how the other party actually approaches negotiating, you'll be in a better position to adjust your methods to their style and perhaps to influence the use of a more cooperative style if necessary.

Recall that when people are taken from their comfort zones, usually by circumstances or events beyond their control, they instinctively react by retreating into whatever behavior pattern will help them get back to that comfort zone again. If the aggressive, power negotiator is removed from his comfort zone by outside factors (like being on unfamiliar turf), he may try to bully and bluster his way into control of the proceedings until he feels comfortable once again.

Similarly, if the passive, shy person is confronted head on, he or she may break off the encounter entirely, preferring to forego the deal rather than suffer the psychological stress he or she associates with negotiating.

Most people get their preconceived notions of how negotiating fits in the world from a variety of outside sources, including childhood experiences, adult-child interactions, adolescent experiences, prior business negotiations, personal dealings, episodes requiring conflict resolution, newspaper and TV news accounts of international negotiations, diplomacy and international relationships, union-management bargaining sessions, and from what they hear secondhand. These impressions add up in their minds and they combine them with their own psychological sense of personal power, self-sufficiency, or the lack of either one.

Much of your success as a negotiator starts with your sensitivity and awareness of how other people have gathered their data about the experience of negotiating. If you make certain valid assumptions based upon what you know about the other party or you can get solid information about their background, it will certainly help you communicate more effectively.

Several centuries ago, the ancient warrior Sun Tzu summed this up when he said, "If you know yourself but not your opponent, you'll win half your battles. If you know your opponent but not yourself, you'll win half your battles. Only when you know yourself and you know your opponent will you win all of your battles."

Even taking this quote out of its obvious adversarial war-related context, the message is still clear: Know what you want and know what the other party wants and strive to get it for both of you. This is the essence of added value negotiating.

THE TESTOSTERONE FACTOR: DO MEN AND WOMEN NEGOTIATE DIFFERENTLY?

Women attend public seminars on negotiating in much smaller numbers than do men. They make up a smaller fraction of the readers of books on negotiating. They are less likely than men to enroll in company training programs on the subject.

Many women who have attended added value negotiating seminars have commented that they find the idea of having to negotiate very distasteful. Because negotiating is an inescapable aspect of our lives, many researchers feel that women are at a disadvantage in such business situations.

A number of feminist business writers have commented on the apparent difference in attitudes that males and females bring to a situation such as a negotiation. Because the Western business world operates largely on male perspectives and values—fewer than 1 percent of corporate chief executives are women—the automatic assumptions and habits that dominate the approach to a negotiation tend to be those of men.

Many men subscribe, consciously or unconsciously, to so-called warrior values in business. The figures of speech they use to describe business operations and business deals are often the metaphors of warfare, combat, tactics, and sport. They often tend to frame business problems in terms of competition and conflict, that is, in doing battle, capturing territory, and winning games and engagements. Males tend to assign lower priorities to issues such as social climate, interpersonal empathy, avoidance of conflict, and human needs than they assign to solving problems, achieving goals, and getting work done.

Many women, probably most, are not fully comfortable with the frame of reference of warfare in many situations. Most have not been accustomed to using the figures of speech of sport in expressing their ideas. They often prefer to frame situations and issues in human and interpersonal terms, not necessarily in "thing" terms. Many women treat the human aspects of a problem on a par with the operational aspects.

Whether these differences are biologically or culturally acquired, or both, is less important than finding ways to reconcile them so that both women and men can feel comfortable and be effective in negotiating fairly and assertively.

Further, the similarities among males and females with regard to negotiating may be greater than the differences, at least for some people. Not all men want to see negotiating as a form of combat. Not all women see it as threatening and combative. There is obviously a certain amount of overlap in views and values, because not all men are the same and not all women are the same. Diversity is a fundamental characteristic of human beings.

Nonetheless, it does seem that more women than men consider negotiating a distasteful experience, and consequently tend to shy away from it or feel reluctant to put their full energies into getting good deals. Many women who have attended AVN seminars have commented that the attitudes, views, and techniques of AVN seem more congruent with a female worldview than the traditional techniques of combat and game playing.

A typical comment of such a person is, "I'm so pleased to discover that there is a way to negotiate that doesn't make me feel I have to conquer someone or be conquered. I can turn everything over to the process. By following the process, and trusting where it takes me, I can eliminate the pushing and shoving, and avoid the battle of wits altogether. I can get something of value, they can get something of value, and there's nowhere near as much stress involved as I expected.''

Perhaps it's fair to say that the AVN approach is neither male nor female in its design. It tends to be somewhat androgynous, appealing to the needs of both genders. Its special appeal for women may be simply that it isn't the standard win-lose approach. It's a method based on maximizing value, not on defeating anybody.

HOW CULTURAL AND NATIONAL DIFFERENCES INFLUENCE NEGOTIATIONS

We all know that a person's ethnical, cultural, or national origin plays a part in forming his or her psychological stance toward negotiating. However, there is such a rich diversity of attitudes, values, beliefs, traditions, and role behavior in various cultures that it seems very dangerous to try to generalize. Very few people have any real depth of experience with more than one country, and in most cases those who do only know one or two cultures beyond their native culture.

It is very difficult to separate truth from fiction, and indeed fiction is where many of us get our impressions of other cultures. Novelists, storytellers, songwriters, comedians, and journalists contribute to the fragmented images, stereotyped patterns, and distorted conceptions of foreigners. We get bits and pieces of emotionally biased information about what it means to be British, American, Australian, Russian, French, German, Italian, Chinese, Japanese, or anybody else.

In what ways do the Chinese negotiate differently from Americans? From Japanese? From Canadians? From Russians? At best, we can only say how some Chinese negotiate, based on reports of people who have negotiated with them. Because very little substantial research has been carried out on this subject, we don't really know whether the typical Italian citizen negotiates very much differently from the typical Mexican citizen. As we've found in various presentations, there are very few things you can say about other cultures that somebody won't challenge, especially somebody who has lived in the country about which you're talking. For this reason, we won't speculate.

Although all cultures have their own variations, it is probably reasonable to generalize so far as to say that most of the European cultures approach negotiating roughly like Americans do, given the common historical origins of many of them. Of course, countries and national governments differ markedly in the degree of sophistication and skill they bring to negotiating.

The social context of the negotiation can have more or less importance, depending on the cultures involved. While Americans and people from other English-speaking countries tend to prefer direct and informal interaction, people from Latin or Asian cultures tend to prefer a higher level of hospitality as a basis for the discussions. In some cases, they consider the host-guest relationship one that must be worked out before the real negotiating begins.

While Americans and other English speakers tend to like to get off the airplane and get right down to business, people from Latin cultures may find this approach too impersonal and somewhat aggressive. In a number of Asian countries, Americans can meet with great frustration when they try the ultradirect approach to business. People who live and work in those ancient business cultures may see negotiation as an implicit, unstated aspect of a long-term relationship, not as a slam-bang problem-solving process.

The quality of the negotiation between nations largely depends upon their historical relationships. The Arabs and the Israelis have hated each other for over 2,000 years. All of that animosity shows up at the bargaining table today. The degree of empathy is very low for these two sides going in and it shows in the negotiating results they fail to achieve. The Chinese and Japanese have been adversaries for many years and through many wars, and yet they have rather practical attitudes regarding their mercantile relationships.

The Finns and the Russians have been glaring at one another for nearly 100 years, and yet they seem to do business somehow. The Americans and Canadians have had the good fortune of being friendly neighbors for many years, and this sets a tone for the way those two countries address their disagreements.

On a more modest scale than international or cultural operations, we have to consider the personal and psychological differences from one culture to another that color negotiations between people themselves. On a commercial level, this relates to what we might call bazaar behavior. There are, in many parts of the world, informal commercial settings in which people do business at the practical, grass-roots level. These are bazaars, flea markets, town squares, and county fairs. All of these situations reflect the values and attitudes of local cultures toward negotiating.

Americans, and to a great extent other English speakers, tend to be a bit uncomfortable in the flea market negotiating context, because they are conditioned from birth to live in a mercantile culture where "the price is the price." One usually doesn't go into a giant supermarket or department store and haggle with the clerk about the price of a dozen eggs or a pair of socks. With minor variations, and with the major exception of large transactions like real estate sales, to an American the first price is the last price. If he or she thinks it's too high, the behavior of choice is to look somewhere else.

But in Bangkok, taxi drivers expect you to negotiate with them. You hail the cab driver and he stops. You tell him where you want to go and ask the fare. He gives you a big grin and says, for example "Three hundred baht." That's probably about twice the going rate. You're supposed to make a counteroffer of about half the going rate, about one-fourth of his figure. Now you've both bracketed the final price. After a few more offers and counteroffers, you've got a deal.

Thai cab drivers aren't money-grubbing rip-off artists, they're Thai cab drivers. What this means is that it's in their cultural nature to bargain. Their culture allows for it and even dictates the way it's done. The result of your negotiating session with the cab driver is that the price ends up being just about what everybody already knows it's supposed to be anyway. The fun is in the bargaining and relationship building that goes on between the cab driver and his prospective passenger.

This is what confuses many Westerners. If you and the cab driver both know it's so many *baht* to get to the Dusit Thani hotel, then why are you negotiating? Because that's how two human creatures establish a sufficient social bond to feel safe and comfortable with each other. It doesn't have to be much of a bond; they don't have to feel like brothers for the rest of their lives, but there is an element of togetherness.

The passenger wants to feel relatively secure about climbing into the back of a vehicle driven by a total stranger, perhaps in an unfamiliar country. The cab driver wants to feel relatively secure about allowing a total stranger from a foreign country to climb into the back of his cab and sit behind him.

Maybe it's no accident that when you get into a taxicab in New York City, you see a solid plexiglas barrier between you and the cab driver, save for a small slot through which you can shove your money through to him. That's the culture for that city and that's what the American culture may teach us about negotiating relationships.

This sensitivity to the context, to the relationship factors, and to the empathy factors involved in human interaction makes people from different countries and different cultural backgrounds negotiate in the ways that make them feel most comfortable. When the native Italian shopkeeper stands very close to you during the conversation about his cheese products, holds on to your forearm, and then gives you a hearty hug at the close of the deal, he's doing what it means to him to negotiate.

When the native Japanese businessman bows to you and then retreats to talk things over with his colleagues, he's following the negotiating rules and practices that influence his culture.

Americans in particular are learning more and more that the American way of negotiating is only one of many ways. Coming from a country so large and so economically powerful, many Yanks have not had to cope with these cultural differences to the extent that people from other countries have. As the day of the dollar fades into the past and Americans see themselves as truly participants in a global relationship of business, they will surely become more aware of the cultural imperatives involved.

THE NEGOTIATING STYLE GRID

While it's not always easy or fair to put labels on people, for the purposes of identifying the traits and tactics of various kinds of negotiators, we've made certain generalizations to help you typecast the people you may encounter across the table.

You've probably dealt with all kinds of people in your negotiating life, ranging from the hard-driving, never-say-die type, to the secretive, guess-my-line type, to the passive, don't-make-waves type.

You can make sense of each of these patterns by looking at two distinctive underlying factors. One is their openness, that is, their willingness to communicate freely without secrecy, to share relatively private information that may be important to that person. The other is their compliance, that is, their willingness to be influenced by what the other person is saying, offering, or suggesting. Using the low and high variations of these two variables, we can identify four different combinations, or styles, as shown in Figure 3–1.

We've slightly exaggerated these styles to help you understand them more thoroughly. Further, most people tend to use a combination of styles, shifting from the dominant one to the fallback, secondary style

FIGURE 3–1
Negotiating Style Grid

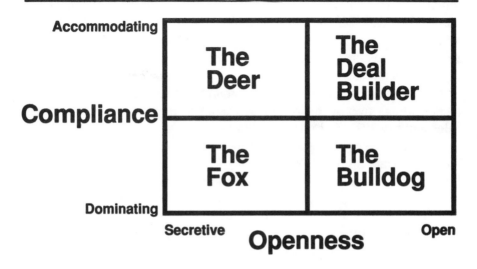

as their response to the negotiation situation changes. Three of these styles are limited in their effectiveness; the fourth is the goal of the added value negotiating approach.

People who display very high openness and very low compliance make it clear from the start that they plan to run right over you. They will usually tell you exactly what they want and will spend their time trying to get it out of you. We call this pattern, or style, the *bulldog*.

People who display very low openness and low compliance don't come straight at you. They rely on tricks, battlefield tactics, and often downright deceit to get what they want from the negotiating session. We call this pattern the *fox*.

People who display low openness but high compliance tend to be those with relatively passive, unassertive personalities, who tend to avoid conflict and confrontation, almost at all costs. We call this pattern the *deer*.

The fourth style, the ideal one from the AVN point of view, models both high openness and high compliance. These people tend to have a greater degree of competence and self-esteem and are more willing to listen to the other party's suggestions and act on them. In an attempt to depart from the animalistic connotations of the other three styles and to move to a more human frame of reference, we call this style the *deal builder*.

The AVN method is essentially the deal builder's marching plan. He or she operates in a negotiating session by telling the other party his or her needs and then goes about meeting those needs, all the while keeping the other person's needs in mind. Deal builders try to understand the other party's situation, mix it with their own, and search for arrangements of value that have joint appeal.

Deal builders have their own recognizable behaviors:

They are strongly motivated by an enlightened self-interest that says, "I'll get a better deal for myself by giving the other party a good deal too."

They work from an honest, impersonal, and systematic view of the situation. Deal builders tend to pay close attention to the process itself, rely on a few basic convictions, and use a few disarmingly simple methods, that is, what we are calling the added value negotiating method.

They concentrate on building quality arrangements of value and offering a selection of options for the other party to analyze and choose, rather than to focus on selling the other party only one deal.

If necessary, they seek to build and preserve future relationships by being fair, empathetic, and creative to the point where the other party would feel comfortable negotiating with them again.

A quick word of caution here: While the deal builder is an open, honest style that seeks to get the best for everyone, it is by no means a "give away the farm" approach. Deal builders can be empathetic toward the other party's needs and still be assertive about meeting their own needs. The deal builder is not a tough negotiator in the accepted sense, but it is very tough to take advantage of such a person.

Although the added value negotiating model concentrates on being fair, it is not designed to let people take advantage of you in your pursuit of a good deal. It also doesn't ask you to put your own needs second but, rather, to be open about your needs and tell the other party you want the best of all worlds—to meet each other's needs and to create a final deal that is completely acceptable to all.

As you review each style, identify the hallmarks of the style, the verbal clues, the motivations of the holder, and the methods by which he or she tries to use the elements of openness and compliance to gain an advantage.

The Bulldog

As negotiators, bulldogs tend to act as follows:

They negotiate by using an aggressive, domineering style; they tend to view a negotiation as a battle of wills.

They consider winning more important than the deal itself. There is often an element of ego identification and self-concept in getting the best of others, and sometimes even in exploiting them.

They use demands, ultimata, and extortion to force you to go along with them. They tend to adopt firm positions and defend them tenaciously. They make concessions grudgingly, if at all, and expect a payoff whenever they do.

One main side effect of negotiating with bulldogs is that you don't feel comfortable with them. Their bombastic approach has a way of turning most people off, which causes animosity and resentment that can cloud the possibility of a good deal.

The Fox

Foxes have their own special behavior patterns that reflect their personal strategies for getting what they want.

They tend to operate from a secretive, manipulative mindset. They force you to guess their motivations and intentions.

Like bulldogs, foxes want the best deal for themselves, but unlike the here-it-comes bulldog, they like to go about getting it in more underground ways. They tend to view a negotiation as a battle of wits rather than a battle of wills.

They often rely on ambiguity, manipulation, and subterfuge to get what they want. You may or may not be able to recognize their tactics when you see them.

They tend to make people who have to negotiate with them feel like they can't trust them, especially if past histories, misstatements, or other unethical behaviors interfere with the negotiation.

The Deer

People with very low openness and very high compliance use the negotiating style of the deer. They don't share with you what they want or what they plan to do. They are very likely to bolt if they get into a threatening situation that takes them out of their comfort zone. People who behave in the deer pattern tend to act as follows:

They choose a passive, accommodating style that doesn't seek to make waves or to antagonize anyone.

They fear conflict or confrontation, sometimes to the point that they cannot negotiate effectively and end up getting their deals handed to them by more aggressive people.

If they do decide to negotiate, they work by evasion or appeasement so as not to upset anyone, themselves or the other party.

They allow the other party to dictate and control the process of the negotiation and tend to acquiesce to the other side's proposals rather than to offer proposals of their own.

They prefer to hide behind surrogates such as business partners, agents, representatives, and intermediaries, who will do the negotiating for them.

This probably describes the majority of the adult negotiating population. Most of us have at least a bit of the deer in us, even though we may feel safer by adopting one of the other patterns. Most of us don't relish hard negotiations and the thought of having to do battle with a pushy car salesperson, a hard-edged realtor, or an aggressive boss takes most of us out of our comfort zones. Many people in this category cheat themselves because they are in such a hurry to get the deal done and get out that they leave too much on the table.

The Deal Builder

The deal builder style is the one recognized by the added value negotiating approach as balancing self-interest with the interests of others. By using both openness and compliance, this person can confidently explore his or her own interests and the options for meeting them, without undue need for secrecy or adversarial behavior.

Studies of effective negotiators suggest that they have evolved a special point of view that reflects the value system and enlightened self-interest associated with what we call the AVN model and philosophy. Although they may not refer to themselves in the terminology of the AVN concept, nevertheless they see themselves as implementing the same precepts.

Deal builders are more comfortable with an all-win approach to negotiating.

They negotiate on the value they can give and get for each deal. They don't waste time focusing on emotional issues, personal attacks, arguments, or personal discussions that sidetrack them from the value elements in a deal.

Deal builders are usually a bit more experienced as thinkers and business people. They're experienced enough to know what is good for them and what is not.

Deal builders have a clear idea what their business interests are, what interests they need to seek, and how to go about meeting those interests by using various options.

They believe in comfort-zone negotiating as a way to develop trust and openness with the other person.

They may not be completely altruistic. They like to see you do well, but they want to do well too.

Deal builders trust the process of openly and collaboratively searching for value because they believe in their instincts and their ability to get a good deal without stooping to bulldog or fox adversarial tactics.

KEY INGREDIENT #4: FLEXIBILITY

Let's consider each of the four different styles as forming a pyramid, with the bulldogs and the foxes sharing the bottom portion; the deer placed in the middle; and the deal builders holding the top position. This hierarchy suggests an upward progression from the more primitive styles, bulldog and fox, through less combative approaches, the deer, to a level of negotiating that goes beyond conflict and combat, the deal builder (i.e., the added value negotiator who can interact effectively with all styles).

Both the bulldog and the fox tend to prey on the deer, that is, their aggressive behavior tends to cause the deer to capitulate and accept inferior deals. When working against each other, the bulldog and the fox tend to fight to a draw. To be an effective deal builder, you must be able to respond effectively to the very different behavior patterns of each.

FIGURE 3–2
The Negotiating Style Hierarchy

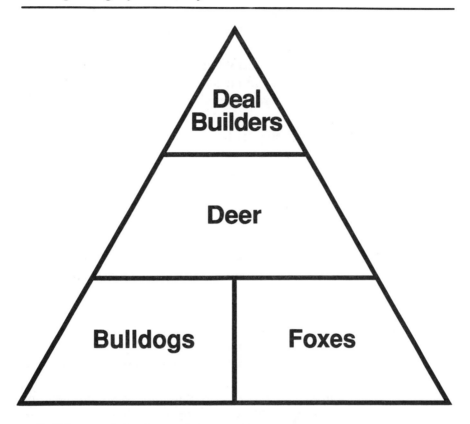

Bulldogs and the foxes of the world probably have the longest way to go to understand the AVN model, because they are at the bottom of the psychological scale of collaborative values. The deer of the world are much more likely to accept the AVN approach because it appeals to their desire to stay within comfort zones.

Although the deer seems to be the style of choice for many people faced with negotiating situations, a delicious irony surrounds the other styles. Why is it that if so many people fall into the deer category, we encounter so many bulldogs and foxes when we negotiate? Bad luck? Murphy's Law? Why do so many of us feel like strapping on helmets and picking up broadswords when we go in to negotiate a simple office lease, a car loan, a business deal, or a personal problem?

Answer: People with deer characteristics tend to regress to the fox, or less likely, the bulldog pattern when they feel insecure or threatened by either of the other two styles.

If you fit the description of a bulldog, chances are that you carry these kinds of traits over into your other personal dealings. If you match the fox pattern, you may tend to operate in a secretive, close-to-the chest fashion outside the negotiating room as well. If you tend to be risk aversive and more oriented toward the idea that "the best way to get along is go along," then you may have the behavior patterns of the deer.

How you are, to put it simply, is how you negotiate: tough and aggressive, secretive and close, passive and accommodating. Win-lose power negotiators tend to be win-lose power people who use aggression as a weapon in their own lives, not just during negotiating sessions. People who are meek and mild in their personal lives tend to be meek and mild in a negotiation.

To continue this personality stereotype even further, let's make even more speculations about the size and shapes that fit each style. Because the bulldog tends to operate in an aggressive way, he or she may even be physically large, intimidating, and more than a little brash. Many people who are sizeable know that they can use their command presence to their advantage. Coupled with the notion that the bulldog may have chosen more physical pursuits in life, he may not be as educated or sophisticated as the fox, who deals more in subterfuge and closeness.

The fox style may be more appealing to well-educated or intellectually-oriented people. They may be more inclined to pride themselves on cleverness, keen insight, and the ability to analyze people and situations.

Keep in mind that while you may have to work harder explaining the added value negotiating model to the bulldogs and the foxes, or convincing them to use it, it may not always be easy to persuade the deer either. Although deer do not usually display any outward signs of aggression, they may have some covert aggression that says, "While I won't make waves like the bulldog, I won't do anything to let you get the better of me."

These people, as accommodating as they may seem, could use passive-aggressive behavior to reaffirm their sense of power over the negotiation. Given this new empowerment, the deer may shift to his or her secondary style as a fox or a closet bulldog.

The fox appears to be a more pivotal negotiating style than the others. If the bulldog feels threatened, put down, or beaten, he or she may shift to the fox style just for a sense of self-protection. If foxes think you're trying to railroad them into accepting this new fangled added value negotiating approach, they may have a tendency to shift into a bulldog mode to protect their flanks.

Research, both before and during the negotiation, may help you pinpoint certain clues to the style of the other party. If you know even a few things about the other person before you start negotiating, you may be able to better classify his or her particular style. This can help you prepare your own approach to meet this style from the context of your own, as a deal builder.

Understanding the other party's negotiating style is not a matter of discovering their weaknesses or coming up with a sneaky way to defeat them. Those notions are not part of the added value negotiating philosophy. You must understand their styles because you will need to adopt methods and processes that avoid their negative side effects and arrive at successful deals.

The following tips will help you negotiate with the bulldogs, foxes, and deer of the world:

Dealing with the bulldog. Question the basis of his or her position; appeal to his or her higher values; and most importantly, don't necessarily respond to his or her outrageous demands. If the bulldog tries to intimidate you with aggressive behavior, don't stand for it. One of the best ways to neutralize that kind of behavior is to recognize it and point it out immediately. If the bulldog tries to dominate the meeting, or attacks you personally, say, "Hey! That's not the way I do business. Let's keep bad feelings or personal attacks out of this. I'm sure you want a good deal just like I do, so let's stick to what we know and agree to find an acceptable deal for both of us."

Often, if you raise your own hackles slightly and specifically point out unacceptable remarks or aggressive behavior, you can ease any building tensions.

Some people are closet bulldogs and some are downright open and proud of it. You'll certainly recognize the up-front bulldogs immediately. Their behavior, conversation, physical or verbal clues, personality, and past reputation will give them away. If you meet with someone who tries to give you a crushing handshake, you can expect to get the bulldog treatment.

While the closet bulldog may not seem dominating at first, he or she can gather momentum as the negotiating situation continues. You may start out with a relatively low-key person, whose true colors show as the negotiation progresses. As noted, some people shift between two negotiating styles. The closet bulldogs may not immediately reveal themselves until you have stated your position. You may have to think fast on your feet and decide with whom you're really dealing.

Here are some more suggestions to help you negotiate with the bulldog:

- Don't personalize or emotionalize the negotiation. Don't take the bulldog's attacks personally. Don't fall victim to putdowns or insults.
- Ask questions about the basis of his or her outrageous claims or demands.
- Keep your eye on the big picture, which is an acceptable deal for both of you.

Dealing with the fox. The best tool you have when dealing with the fox is information. The more you know, the more you can clear the air and neutralize attempts at trickery or deceit. The fox's tricks usually work only if you're caught unaware or don't have enough information to know better. You may have to use some careful information-gathering questions to clarify the basis of the interests involved and the conditions surrounding the negotiation.

The more you know, the more you can study his or her position and ask yourself questions like "Why would he look at things that way?" or "What is her motivation for that statement?" Instead of using your information to find a weak point, like the typical power negotiators would do, take the information you learn, refer to your own needs, and invite the fox to be more constructive and more involved in creating a deal you both like.

Here are some suggestions to help you negotiate with the fox:

- Don't personalize or emotionalize the negotiation. Focus on information: interests, value, options, and rational support for various exchanges of value.
- Gather as much information as you can about the other party's needs and use a number of fact-finding questions to draw him or her out.
- Search for the fox's hidden agenda. You may even find it's surprisingly similar to your interests.

- Let it be known up front that you seek to create the best deal for both of you and try to encourage more openness and compliance by modeling it yourself.
- Keep your eye on the big picture, which is an acceptable deal for both of you.

Dealing with the deer. These people are usually the easiest to approach and negotiate with because in most cases you're not dealing with aggression. The main thing you must do is create a comfort zone for this person. With the deer, the AVN approach has great appeal because it is a comfort-zone method from the start.

Once they see you are offering an honest, transparent, cards-on-the-table system, they feel much more comfortable, less likely to leave, and more ready to create a deal. Once the deer trusts you, sees your credibility, and knows that you plan to negotiate around value, then he or she will probably settle back and help you get a deal that serves both of you.

High-pressure tactics only force the deer into a shell. The tricks and gimmicks of either the bulldog or the fox only make things worse. The deer is most likely to flee the scene or close up and not make any decisions about anything. If you're dealing with someone who constantly says, "Let me think it over and get back to you," and they sincerely mean it, you're probably working with the deer. These people are often uncomfortable about making a critical decision and even more so if they feel backed into a corner or challenged by aggression.

If they can't decide, maybe they need more space from you. Because most people have been victims of the hard sell at least once in their lives and because most people fall under the category of the deer, it's easy to see why deer may feel the most negotiator's remorse after closing a deal.

Nissan, the Japanese car manufacturer who makes the Infiniti model, has seen the light when it comes to creating comfort zones for people. Realizing that most people typically do not enjoy the sales process when buying a new car, they have softened the event by replacing the standard high-pressure sales force.

Now when you enter an Infiniti showroom, you're invited to walk around and look at the cars, enjoy a cup of coffee or tea, and read the brochures describing the models. When you're ready, you can signal a sales associate who will answer your questions. Infiniti does not follow the pattern of most car sales firms, who allow deal-hungry sales people to chase you all around the lot in an effort to "put you in the car today."

Knowing that people may have had bad experiences in the past, especially when it comes to negotiating the price, this car seller has adjusted the entire approach to buying and selling a car. Because they realize they're selling a high-end foreign-made luxury automobile, the Infiniti people have transformed their organization into a service-oriented, low-key place that caters to the deer of the world. This, indeed, is becoming the trend in automobile marketing.

Here are some more suggestions to help you negotiate with the deer:

- Keep the deer within the comfort zone. Try to be forthright in your explanations, up front with your desire to meet certain needs, and clear about how you see his or her position.

- Reassure him or her constantly that you are only interested in a good deal for all concerned, not in winning the negotiation.

- Monitor your vocabulary and terminology carefully, being sure to avoid typical battlefield phrases and high-pressure sales expressions that may lead the other party to conclude you're a win-lose power negotiator.

- Explain each part of the AVN model thoroughly. Answer any questions and be ready to stop and discuss things if he or she needs more reassurance.

- Model openness and compliance, asking the other person to do the same. If the deer feels more empowered, perhaps he or she will fully participate in the mutual search for a good deal.

Flexibility. The problem with both the bulldog and the fox is that their personalities may serve to contaminate their thinking. In some cases, winning the negotiation is more important than getting a good deal. They may take a deal that has less value all around just to get the feeling that they have conquered somebody. While this may sound paradoxical, some bulldogs and foxes will virtually sabotage a negotiation just to claim victory, even though the resulting deal is not good for either party.

In these difficult situations, it may take more time for you to convince them that greater value is more important in the deal than victory. You must be patient and have a practical sense in your own mind of what really can be achieved. In some cases where you must deal with an affirmed bulldog, it just may not be possible to get a good deal at that time.

If you're dealing with an unreasonable person, you may leave. Sometimes you must say, "It looks like we just can't do business together. Maybe next time."

Some skeptics will say that you should never back out of a deal, especially when you have something important to gain or to lose. Labor union and management people often take this approach, chaining themselves to the bargaining table for hours and hours just to spend their time berating one another, hashing over the same points, and trying to extract concessions. Maybe the better tack in this potential no-win situation would be for both sides to adjourn and reschedule after they've had more time to analyze their respective positions with the other party in mind.

When you're dealing with bulldogs and foxes, don't get hooked by their aggression. If they approach you in a negative way, don't respond in kind. If they use aggressive behavior, don't return the favor. Deflect it, just like a judo player will allow his opponent to come at him at full speed and then redirect his momentum. No matter how the other party acts (short of physical violence) you should continue to model positive, added value behaviors.

All this is not to say that you cannot like the bulldog or the fox as people; you just may not agree with the way they negotiate. These descriptions represent the extreme ends of the negotiating spectrum. The bulldog does not literally snarl and bare his or her teeth, cause a scene, or seek to physically overpower you. The description of the bulldog matches the way he or she negotiates—aggressively and with domination in mind.

While the fox does not literally wear a trenchcoat and sunglasses into the room, talk in secret codes, or use riddles to make you guess what he or she wants, there is an element of secrecy (close-to-the-chest mindset) that makes it hard for you to figure out what he or she wants in a deal.

The deer may not venture timidly into the room waiting for you to capture him or her, but deer do not always assert their interests and may not feel comfortable with any high-pressure negotiating tactics.

In some respects, the sheer innocence of the added value negotiating approach may throw the bulldogs and the foxes for a loop. These people usually expect you to respond to their negotiating style in kind. When you don't, it can take the edge off their aggression, and it can appeal to the deer for the very same reasons.

Ultimately, your strategy should be to reduce the power involved to the power of value. Always remember:

Value is the ultimate power in any negotiation.

Dealing with deal builders. While the deal builder's style is mutually beneficial, it also has a natural degree of self-protectiveness in it. The deal builder is happy to see you do well, but he or she is not about to give up the ranch just to make you happy.

Putting two deal builders together may help to dramatically shorten the amount of time spent negotiating, as well as diminish much of the inherent feeling-out "processes" that go on before and during any negotiating session. This is not to say that all deal builders are perfect, but rather that they tend to enter the negotiation process better equipped to find a mutually acceptable deal. More than any other style, deal builders bring a careful match of assertiveness and fairness to the table.

Chapter Four

Self-Interest
The Great Engine of All Behavior

IT ALWAYS HELPS PROVE
HOW RIGHT YOU ARE

IF YOU
WAVE YOUR ARMS
AND JUMP
AND SCREAM.

Ashleigh Brilliant, © Brilliant Enterprises, 1974.

The first step in the added value negotiating process is clarifying the interests of all parties involved. Using careful research, diagramming tools such as the window of interest, and a disciplined meet-and-confer cycle, you can create a solid basis for everything else that follows in the negotiation.

As Figure 4–1 illustrates, it is important to understand three critical components of a negotiation: the context in which it takes place, the relationship between the parties, and the value involved in the exchange. We will deal with each of these three elements throughout this book.

UNDERSTANDING THE CONTEXT
OF THE NEGOTIATION

Every human interaction takes place in some context or other. There is no such thing as communication, of any kind, between two people, that is

FIGURE 4–1

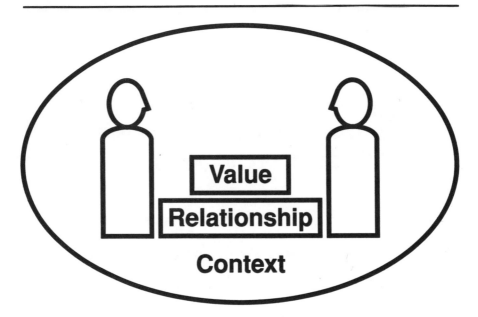

not affected by the context in which the two parties interact. Whether it's in an office, at a party, on an airplane, in someone's home, at a wedding, at a funeral, or over the telephone, there is always a context. Even if you could imagine two people communicating in outer space, that's still their own context.

A context is a setting in which something happens and that affects the psychological meaning of the event. Context always contributes something to the interaction between people. By paying attention to context, you can understand what's really happening to them.

When a husband and wife who are going through a divorce appear in front of a judge, the formal legal context of the situation allows for very little in the way of a free exchange of ideas. When they meet in the office of a marriage counselor, it's a different context and their behaviors will be different. If they meet in their home, in the presence of their children, it's yet another context.

Every context has rules for behaving. Some behaviors are acceptable in church, others are acceptable in a restaurant, and others are acceptable at a meeting of the United Nations Security Council.

Every negotiation takes place within a context. If it involves a series of meetings, the context can vary from one meeting to the next. The location of a meeting, the physical facility, the people who are there, the agenda, the procedures, and the onlookers are all part of the context.

Each negotiating context has an invisible part as well. When representatives of two countries get together to discuss a matter between them, they bring all of their history with them. Their history is part of the context. Their individual cultural values, their attitudes toward each other, and any prior positions they may have taken on the issue at hand are all part of the context.

If the negotiation between them is important to others, then the fact that there are onlookers is critical to the context. A United Nations meeting is a very different context from a meeting in a hotel conference room. If there are journalists and photographers hanging on every word and every photo opportunity, that is an important element of the context.

If it is a critical labor negotiation between company representatives and union chiefs and a strike is impending, the presence of journalists can often tempt one or the party to negotiate on TV, by making claims and accusations about the other party. When the journalists and camera operators go to the other party to get a rebuttal, they become part of the negotiating context, and indeed part of the negotiation itself.

An important part of the thinking process of added value negotiating is a consciousness of the context of the negotiation, and a conscious effort to manage that context. This also connects with the importance of maintaining empathy between the parties. It is possible, and important, to negotiate about negotiating, i.e., to jointly decide about important elements of the context, which may strongly influence the behavior of the parties involved.

For example, both parties might agree not to make statements to the press during a certain period. This would be an important decision about the context. They might decide to alternate the location of the meetings, first at the quarters of one party and then at the other's. They might decide to engage the services of a third-party facilitator or mediator; this could have a huge effect on the context of the negotiation.

As we go deeper into the discussion of the methods of added value negotiating, keep in mind the critical importance of the context of any negotiation and resolve to manage the context just as carefully and consciously as you tend to all the other critical elements of the process.

CONSTRAINTS AND GROUND RULES: NEGOTIATE ABOUT NEGOTIATING

You can build a solid foundation for the negotiating process at the outset by paying attention to the how even before you begin working on the what. By getting agreement with the other party about the general course of the negotiation and any important parameters that have to be involved, you can save both parties time, effort, and possibly frustration. By setting constraints and ground rules, you can channel all of the energies involved more productively.

Think of a constraint as either a restriction or a requirement imposed on the value options by one party's needs in the situation. Think of a ground rule as a requirement the parties choose to impose on the negotiating process itself. Let's consider each of them further.

A constraint affects the possible ingredients of the deal packages the two parties might consider. For example, a married couple negotiating a divorce might agree at the outset that any settlement must provide for their children's attendance at a private school. This provision must be a part of any deal they agree to, so there is no point in treating it as an option in designing deal packages. It is a common item that must appear in all deals.

Similarly, one party to a business negotiation may desperately need cash to solve his or her problem, so a noncash deal is not an option. In a labor negotiation, the union leaders might make it clear that they will not propose any settlement to their members that has the appearance of a give-back and significantly reduces their entitlement in any one area. The company representatives may insist that any deal they consider must contain provisions for union support of productivity improvement programs.

In each case, one or more of the parties simply will not accept any deal package that does not account for their critical factor. Such a factor is a constraint on the negotiating process. Whoever puts together the various deal packages for consideration needs to account for those constraints. Overlooking them will be a waste of time.

Bear in mind, however, that too many constraints placed on the negotiation at the beginning can severely limit the possibilities for creatively adding value. When one or more of the players imposes a number of stringent constraints, then at some point the deal-design process has already begun, and begun badly at that. When the owner of the restaurant says to the prospective buyer, "I won't take less than X for the business," he or she may be limiting the possibilities too soon. Why not hear what the buyer has to say? It's easy to say no to any unacceptable deal package, but you can't turn down an option that never arises.

It's important to identify constraints at the outset, but it's just as important to limit the constraints to those absolutely essential to your needs, and not foreclose creative options that may arise during the process of designing deals. Each party can consider carefully, during the stage of clarifying interests, what situational factors are truly critical, and how they translate into constraints. Beyond these few essential constraints, virtually all options for an exchange of value are at least worthy of consideration.

Ground rules, on the other hand, deal with the negotiating process itself. They are provisions that help to clarify roles, procedures, and rules for estimating the value of various options. A very simple ground rule might relate to the time span of the negotiation. For example, both parties might agree that they will either come to an agreement or terminate the negotiation by a certain date. This ground rule could give them both the opportunity to take advantage of other courses of action on a timely basis.

It is often wise to agree on ground rules about who represents the various parties. In a divorce negotiation, does each spouse speak on his or her own behalf, or does all communication go through their legal representatives? Does the person you've been communicating with actually have the authority to accept a deal? Or will it be necessary for him or her to take one or more deal packages to a higher authority for consideration?

The parties involved might agree on a ground rule about where their meetings will take place. They might alternate, with each one hosting the other in turn. Or they might agree to meet in some convenient location accessible to both.

Some ground rules might be more technical. For example, two companies considering a merger might agree on certain accounting procedures or reference sources they will use to value the assets involved. This is a ground rule for the process. It will prevent arguments when they get to the critical stage of evaluating the various deal packages they are working with.

In a complex technical negotiation, both parties might agree to have a neutral third-party consultant or technical expert present at all major meetings to provide technical advice. They might agree to share the expense of having the advisor there. This becomes a ground rule for the negotiation.

Don't confuse ground rules with constraints, and be sure to use both sparingly. A ground rule governs the negotiating process itself, while a constraint applies to the various elements of value eligible for inclusion in the deal packages you will design.

If the negotiation is even moderately complex, it is a good idea to include specific statements of constraints and ground rules when you document the interests involved. A simple but effective method for this is to draft a memorandum or letter of understanding covering the respective interests of the parties involved and identifying the constraints and ground rules. This can become a useful guideline that can keep the negotiating process moving forward effectively.

OPENNESS, HONESTY, AND EMPATHY: THE PARADOXICAL POWER OF TRANSPARENCY

Tell them nothing about yourself, what you need, or what you're willing to give up.

This is the kind of advice people typically get in conventional negotiating seminars. This is one of the most destructive rules imaginable. Conversely, one of the most important and fundamental parts of the added value negotiating model centers around sharing and understanding interests—yours and the other party's.

The more you know about your own interests, the more you know about the other party's interests, and the more information you share with each other about your respective interests, the better deal you will create in the end. This flies right in the face of everything the tough, power negotiators teach in their books, articles, and training seminars.

Typical win-lose negotiations reduce the value of the deal because each side takes away things rather than gives them. By holding back potentially important information, each side will struggle to reach an agreement that doesn't violate one or more of their respective value areas. It's like playing darts in the dark. You just may hit the board with a lucky toss, but the chances are better that you'll continue to miss by a wide margin because you don't know where to aim.

If you don't understand the other side's interests, then you'll also end up stabbing around in the dark without any clear idea of what appeals to them or even what to propose. It sounds like one of the most obvious things in the world, but people often enter negotiation sessions with only the vaguest idea about what they want or what the other side wants. It's as if they hope the answers to these critical elements will appear as if by magic if they just spend enough time at the negotiating table.

Let's drop in on a negotiating seminar—one of the more well-known negotiating training programs on the market today. As an exercise during the program, each person gets a role play scenario to act out with another member of the class. One person is to assume the role of a desperate owner of a fruit warehouse. If he doesn't buy a large semitrailer very soon, all of his produce will spoil and he will lose thousands of dollars. The other person plays the part of a desperate semi-truck owner who needs fast cash to pay off a balloon note on his vehicle. If he doesn't get the money, he will lose his truck to the bank.

When the role play session began, each party followed the rules of the engagement: Don't give up any more information than necessary, find out all you can about the other person by asking a lot of questions, and try to get the best deal for yourself.

As a result, several people in the room got into shouting matches with their opponents. Other groups played cat and mouse so effectively that by the end of the time limit, neither one could agree on a deal. The conclusive part of this tale started after each person revealed his or her true needs to the other. Cries of "If I had known that was what you needed, I could have easily helped you out" filled the room. Some people were visibly upset that the "rules" of this "game" did not allow them to negotiate like real human beings.

Let's dissect this so-called negotiating exercise ourselves. What basic interests does the owner of the fruit have?

1. Get his fruit out of his warehouse and to his produce distributors as soon as possible.
2. Get a reliable transportation method he can use to continue in business.
3. Keep his transportation costs in line with his revenue and other costs, so he can operate profitably.

How about the truck owner? What interests does he have?

1. Get at least enough cash to pay off his balloon note as soon as possible.
2. Keep his truck if possible.
3. Continue working in the trucking business.

What might have happened if the fruit warehouse owner had told the truck owner of his problem? What might have happened if the truck owner had told the fruit warehouse owner of his problem? Do you see where the interests of each dovetail together in certain areas? If communication between the two parties had been allowed, they might have created a fair deal for both of them.

Instead of this constant preoccupation with focusing on weak points, i.e., he needs a truck badly, so I can cheat him on the price, or he needs to get fast cash, so I can make him a ridiculously low offer, why not focus your efforts on solving the other party's problems as you solve your own? You do that by outlining your interests and those of the other party, not in secret, but right up front as a part of the added value negotiating process.

Who is to say that by exploiting the other person's fear, apprehension, or sense of urgency, that you will get a better deal? Why not be direct and say, "Here's what I need and here's what I think you might need. Correct me if I'm wrong about your needs, but I'm ready to start talking about solving problems for both of us."

Offering value is the key to the AVN method. Searching for weaknesses and making the other person come to you on your own terms while he or she seeks to hide weak points is no way to create or continue a healthy, long-term negotiating relationship.

We've discussed the need for empathy within the AVN model. It's hard to define this abstract concept because it's more something you feel rather than something you do. There is no bona fide prescription that helps you become empathetic. It's a process that brings you closer to the other person as a unique individual, and more in tune with his or her needs as the other party in a negotiation. It's not something you can dictate but rather a state of affairs that you can create and manage with your behavior.

Openness and honesty in any negotiation have two values: (1) they contribute to the development of empathy between the two parties and (2) they have utilitarian value in helping with the exchange of information.

Empathy is not just related to individuals; it can exist between groups, organizations, nations, and any entities that come together seeking to negotiate.

In the added value negotiating context, openness, honesty, and empathy can give you more power than you ever thought possible. The more you give of yourself by adding value to the deal, the more you'll get in return.

But some of those negotiating graybeards still believe that you're in jeopardy of losing the battle if your opponent learns too much about your interests. How could this hurt your bargaining position if you maintain the AVN context? This is an open question. Recall the fruit warehouse–semitrailer example. If either one of those parties had put the cards on the table and said, "Look, in all honesty I'm kind of up against it. I need to sell my fruit or sell my truck. . . . "

One guy needs to get his fruit to market or he will lose more than just money. His reputation with his customers, distributors, grocers, and so forth is on the line as well. How about the financial needs of his employees in the warehouse? How much face could he possibly lose by being open and honest with the truck owner?

How about the truck owner? What if he said, "Listen, I have a pressing need to sell my truck. Let's not haggle back and forth about the price. Let me tell you what I need to help my financial situation and let's see if we can settle on that as a fair price."

What interests does the truck owner have besides settling with the bank? He certainly wants to protect his credit rating, keep his bank happy in case he wants to make a deal with them in the future, and protect his reputation in the trucking industry. How much face would he lose by being open and honest with the fruit-warehouse owner?

In a worst case scenario, the fruit-warehouse owner may think he has the trucker over a barrel over the price of the truck, but you could apply the same reasoning to the trucker, who might think he could hold out for a higher price because of the warehouse owner's need to ship his product.

Experience suggests something different, however. In this deal, which is not unlike the millions of other negotiations going on right this minute, if both sides are honest with each other, they will quickly see how they can add more value to the deal than originally thought possible and save the day for everyone involved.

Thanks to the flexibility of the AVN model in terms of the hundreds of options both sides could produce, the chances of either party cheating the other seems remote.

By modeling openness and compliance, you're actually empowering yourself and you're adding to the success of the AVN model. While this may sound like a naive view of the business world to the hardbitten negotiator, it proves itself time after time.

You can't go about getting a good deal for yourself if you don't know what you want. As logical and obvious as that sounds, scores of people go into complicated negotiations with only the vaguest idea of what interests they want to meet. Trying to get by on wits alone is a good way to blow an important deal. We've seen people come to the negotiating table armed with only a smile and a handshake. Some folks don't even bring a pen with them!

If you're going to make a quick deal—for the sale of some small item, for example—then it's not necessary to bring reams of paper and make a huge production out of a matter that doesn't require it. Similarly, if you plan to negotiate anything of substance—whether it's an important business deal, a critical personal event, or a problem involving other people, many moving parts, and different directions—it's not wise to come in unprepared.

At the least you'll need a pen and a pad so you can be ready to capture and analyze critical information in detail. Trying to rely on your memory can cause you to leave out important steps or forget to ask critical questions. If the negotiating situation is especially stressful, then you have even more opportunities to make mistakes.

One of the best ways to clarify your interests is to make a written list of them. When you see them on paper, it will improve your ability to organize them and later to communicate them to the other party. If you're dealing with a power negotiator on an important matter, you can bet he or she will have a list of demands at the ready.

One of the key words in the AVN model is *clarify*. With a written list of your interests and those of the other party, you can stop midway and say, "Before we start looking at actual deals that we can create, do I understand that these are your interests?"

Showing the other party your list of mutual interests goes a long way toward building empathy between you. It tells the other person that you have listened to his or her interests, made note of them, and compared them with your own.

Don't Confuse Interests with Options

While almost everyone who learns the AVN method understands the model immediately, a few people have trouble fully appreciating the differences between interests and options.

Interests, as you'll recall from the definition in Chapter 2, are unique needs, desires, aspirations, or outcomes that the parties to a negotiation seek to satisfy.

Options, you'll remember, are not the same as interests; they are ways to satisfy interests. Options are various ways of packaging the elements of value involved in a negotiation. One is very different from the other.

For more clarification, look at these examples of these interests and their respective options:

Interest. Develop a long-term relationship with the other party.
Option. Draft a five-year lease.

Interest. Get protection from competition.
Option. Get worldwide rights to sell the product.

Interest. Get a good price for my house.
Option(s). $100,000; $125,000; $150,000.

Interest. Maintain high property values in the area.
Option. Enforce a set of neighborhood rules and regulations.

Interest. Keep inventory costs low.
Option. Have the seller hold the inventory until we need it.

If you'll recall the physical model that makes up the window of interest, it's divided into "what we want" and "what they want." Subjective or intangible interests make up one part and objective or tangible interests make up the other.

Subjective interests are intangible or abstract. You can hold the title to a piece of property in your hands (objective, tangible), but you cannot physically hold the concept of goodwill (subjective, intangible). Keep these differences in mind as you and the other party develop the window of interest. In all of the conversations and verbal back and forth movements that go on in a typical negotiation, it's sometimes hard to keep the interests and options separate in your mind. Don't confuse the two as you go through the AVN process.

Interests are things you wish to satisfy; options are ways to satisfy them. Being rich, for example, is an interest. Winning the state lottery is one option that can meet that interest. Of course, if we want to be semantically correct, we have to acknowledge that every interest is also an option for attaining some higher-level interest. Being rich, for example, can be an option for some more abstract interest, such as being happy, or being free from certain cares or obligations.

All of negotiation can serve one or more of three objectives: (1) meet a need, (2) solve a problem, or (3) add value. Why else would a person sit down with another person and try to make a deal? If you discover which of these important three goals pertains to the other party, either before you begin to negotiate or during the process, you'll be in a much better position to add value to your deal.

Sometimes all three of these goals are important to the other side, but most people come into a negotiation wanting to meet a pressing need or to solve a pressing problem. Rather than using your knowledge of these needs or problems to take supreme advantage, as the win-lose power brokers would strongly urge, why not become a deal builder and add value instead?

"Confession," says the old adage, "is good for the soul." When you model openness and honesty by saying, "Here are the needs I have and here are the problems I'm trying to solve," you start the negotiation from the deal builder's position.

The Window of Interest: What We Want and What They Want

As previously explained in Chapter 2, the window of interest is a simple but very powerful pen-and-paper tool you can use to get your negotiation going effectively. Indeed, it's a key element of the AVN process. It's something you can draw on the back of a paper placemat in a restaurant or present as part of a formal communication process between two negotiating parties. Figure 4–2 illustrates the relationship between what "we want" and what "they want," with each of them further divided into objective interests and subjective interests.

Remember that objective interests are those you can express in tangible form. They involve things like cash, measurable profit, securities, personal property, real estate, equipment, valuable data or information, and physical security.

Subjective interests are those that require human judgment for their evaluation. These may be good health, copyrights and trademarks, rights

FIGURE 4–2
Using the Window Of Interest—Example

We want:	They want:
Subjective interests (judgmental) • Protect our reputation • Good working relationship • Market opportunities	• Low business risk • Credibility in markets • Protect image
Objective interests (measurable) • Cash ASAP • Low interest rate • Quick response • Long-term relationship	• Safety of capital • Specific marketing rights • No competition

to use brand identities, good will, peace of mind, preservation of one's business reputation, and freedom from financial risk.

You may find that the subjective interests in a particular situation are more numerous and more diversified than the objective interests. After you've enumerated the money and property factors, you may run out of tangibles rather quickly, but as you discuss the possibilities in the deal with the other party, you may find you keep discovering more and more areas of common or congruent interest, quite beyond the tangible ones.

The window of interest model, used either informally or formally, can serve as a very useful tool for communicating about interests. During the preliminary getting-to-know-you discussions with the other party, you can simply pull out a notepad and a pen and start filling in the four blocks or panes of the window model as the discussion proceeds. It's not even necessary to refer to what you're doing, although you'll almost certainly discover that the diagram catches the other person's interest.

How large your window of interest is depends upon several factors: the complexity of the negotiating issue, the amount of time you have to negotiate with the other party, and his or her willingness to share information and communicate effectively. While you may not have much control over the first two—complexity and deadlines—you may be able to influence the third—honest communication. If you approach the negotiation in a detached, professional manner, modeling openness and expressing a desire to be honest about what you want, this may have an enormous effect on the other party.

Once you've exhausted the interests on both sides and your window of interest is complete, go back and review the list to find the areas where you and the other party share common ground. If you don't share any mutual interests, you may have to go back and refine the mutual search process even further. You and the other person don't need to agree on everything; his or her interests may be vastly different from yours. However, you should share at least some of the same interests to come up with the best deals possible.

Throughout the early stages of the process and during the meet-and-confer cycle, if you have a number of meetings, keep filling out and clarifying the window of interest. At some point, you'll probably have it clear enough to be able to discuss it with the other party and more or less formally ratify it. If you put the agreed version of it on paper and give it an official appearance, you can use it as a tool for discussion and for guiding the negotiation as it proceeds.

By showing the other party that you're willing to do business in a fair manner and explaining your desire to engage in a mutual search for value, you may be able to make him or her feel more relieved about the actual negotiation process. With less pressure and a promise from you to communicate fully and negotiate fairly, many people will feel more comfortable about volunteering information that you need to understand their interests.

The other advantage of the window of interest, of course, is that it serves as the primary litmus test of any deal package that emerges from the discussion. When you have developed several alternative deal packages, by whatever means the parties find acceptable, you can weigh them against the items shown on the window of interest. It should be the final arbiter of the value of all deal packages.

Once you have the interests clearly defined and expressed to the satisfaction of all parties as a window diagram, you are ready to analyze the elements of value available in the deal. The better you have defined the interests, the better job you'll be able to do in defining value and identifying options for packaging it.

When you've created the window and identified the areas of mutual interest, you're ready to move on to the second step in the AVN model—identifying options that will meet your needs and those for the other party.

Questioning and Listening to Discover Interests

People with excellent communication skills, both verbal and written, tend to negotiate better because they know what to ask, when to ask it, what to say, and how to say it. Because they can accurately capture their thoughts on paper, they have a written record of their desires, the needs of the other party, and their mutual interests.

If you're having problems in your negotiations, you might start by taking a closer look at the way you listen to people. While this may sound like teaching the choir to sing, listening is a high-skill activity.

For most people, the opposite of talking is not listening, but simply waiting for a chance to talk again. Learn to listen intently and actively, by paraphrasing what the other person has said and filling in what you don't know, that is, "Mr. Jones, if I heard you correctly, what you hope to achieve is. . . ."

Active listening
1. Be open and receptive with your body language.
2. Hear all of what the other person says before you respond.
3. Don't interrupt or finish sentences for the other person.
4. Interpret the other person's message by listening for feelings as well as facts.
5. Act on what he or she has said.

Before you even start any negotiating session, warm up your paraphrasing skills first. "Paraphrasing," according to George Thompson, creator and leader of the "Verbal Judo" seminar, "is a necessary backup system to communication. It means putting the other person's 'meaning' into your 'words' and then giving it back to him or her."

This technique of replaying what the other person has said and putting it into your own words can pay powerful dividends during any negotiation. Besides the obvious way it helps you organize and clarify your own thoughts, it will build immediate rapport with the person.

Paraphrasing allows you to get the information right the first time. The other person can correct you if you've made an error, and the paraphrased statement makes him or her feel better because it "mirrors back" what he or she originally said to you.

"It also," says Thompson, "makes the other person a better listener to you. No one will listen harder than to his or her own point of view."

Paraphrasing also has a tendency to create more empathy between you and the other party; the person will believe you are really trying to understand what he or she is all about.

Besides good active listening skills, a pen and a piece of paper can be powerful negotiating tools in the right hands. Taking good notes, creating the window of interest and the option tree, and listening actively signals a certain strength to the other party. In a nonverbal way, it demonstrates that you're serious about the negotiation, committed to modeling the AVN method, and won't allow any mistakes, omissions, or communication problems get in the way of creating a good deal.

If the other person asks what you're doing—as a win-lose negotiator might do in an accusatory fashion—say, "I don't want to make any mistakes. I want to capture what you've said here on paper so I can refer to it later. Any deal we make will be tested against these criteria."

Your list of interests is much like fresh concrete. While in its early stage, you can move it and shape it to your liking. As time goes on, however, it begins to solidify and acquire a sense of permanence. In the early stages of your negotiation, you can add or delete interest items as much as you think necessary, until you and the other person have exhausted the realm of possibilities. As the session progresses, you should begin to focus on tightening the list of interests to match the negotiation criteria.

As an example, when the other party wants $500,000 for his house, which may be an interesting option, but the house was appraised at $250,000, he should be ready to present why he thinks the house is worth that price.

How you question the other party demands careful forethought. Keep in mind that you're not conducting a police interrogation; you're attempting to gather information in a professional, humane, and efficient manner.

Besides the information you receive, you're also testing the situation for empathy. If you have built even the slightest positive rapport with him or her, answers will come more freely than if you start the relationship under a pretense of suspicion, caution, or mistrust. If the other person feels a developing sense of empathy in the air, he or she will usually be much more forthcoming with answers to your questions.

This only makes sense. We talk freely with people we trust and not to those we don't. The hardnosed negotiator who tries to steamroll you from the start will not get much helpful information if you feel threatened, put down, or defensive. Even if the bulldog were to see the error of his or her ways (which seems doubtful in most cases) and try to make amends, no amount of false compliments can recover from this bad beginning.

While careful questioning can help you understand the other party's interests and serves as an empathy-building device, it also acts as a bulldog-detector or a fox-locator. In most cases, you'll know immediately whom you're dealing with based on their responses to your questions or the lack thereof. Bulldogs will usually let you know they mean business by trying to take over the question-and-answer role. Foxes will be less visible and also less forthright in their answers. Either way, careful, even casual, questions from you can quickly gauge either style.

In more complex situations, your first encounter with the other person is not really a meeting to negotiate, it's a meeting to discover things. You may move from phone conversations and correspondence to an actual face-to-face session. As with most situations relating to encounters between human beings, you will rely on gut feelings to tell you if the other party appears reasonably honest, straightforward, and willing to do a deal in a fair manner.

You try to see where you are, where the other party is, and what mutual interests you may have. As suggested in the discussion of the meet-and-confer cycle, don't always try to close the deal in the first session, especially if it involves many complex parts, high-asset figures, or research chores that you or the other party still may need to accomplish.

If a negotiation is going on between two companies, for a merger or a joint product effort perhaps, both sides should leave the initial meeting (provided they can all be at least cordial to one another) with some accurate sense of where their respective interests lie. Based on that first encounter, some of the more literate members of either party can draft a document that outlines what the first meeting covered, that is, "Based on our discussions, we think these are the interests of our corporation and these are the interests of yours. If we understand these interests correctly, may we proceed to the next phase in the negotiation?"

While simple issues may require only a quick initial meeting to clarify the interests on both sides, more complicated matters may require days or even weeks of study. The more you need to know, the more work you'll have to put in to get to the next stage of the AVN model, identifying options.

If you look at negotiation as a whole, remember that you operate from one context and the other party operates from another. It may stem from a business matter, a personal issue, or combinations of both. You may have a conflict to resolve and need to serve as the intermediary between two parties. Your intention is to make sure that whatever takes place during the negotiation contributes value from within those contexts.

When you ask the other person, "What are your interests?" you may not get enough information of quality to help you evaluate him or her. While you can't say, "Tell me all about your life, where you're coming from, and where you're going," that is, in reality, much of what you're trying to find out to skillfully meet your interests and those of the other person.

What's going on in the other person's life or business situation that relates to you can become interests to discuss. We're not suggesting that you ask prying personal questions that put the other person on the spot or make him or her defensive, but we are saying that if you want to make the best deal for both of you, you should know where that person is coming from and why. His or her interests, matched with yours, become inputs into the total negotiation process.

Chapter Five

Finding Value in Every Negotiation
The Option Tree

Ashleigh Brilliant, © Brilliant Enterprises, 1974.

Now that you've completed the first step of clarifying interests, you are ready to move on to the challenging step of analyzing the different elements of value that are possible in the negotiation and identifying options for each. This will enable you to respond to each of the interests with appropriate combinations of options and thereafter help you to design effective deal packages. This second step of the added value negotiating process calls for identifying options.

THE FIVE VALUE FACTORS IN EVERY NEGOTIATION

Like beauty, value is in the eye of the beholder, "One man's trash is another man's treasure," and so forth. What you perceive as a valuable part of the deal may mean absolutely nothing to the other party. Conversely, what may not be at all important to you may have significant value to the other party.

Win-lose practitioners contend that you should use this kind of trade-off information as a weapon.

If you should succeed in getting this information, according to the win-losers, either through conversations, by accident, or through dedicated research—you can tilt the negotiation in your favor and use it as an effective bargaining chip. They preach that if you know or discover that the other party needs or wants something that you could just as well add to the deal for free, don't do it! They believe that with this new ammunition in hand, you're in a better position to get something that you want by holding onto that value item. All's fair in trade and war, they say.

When the added value negotiator, however, learns of something the other party wants, he or she doesn't hold that item as "hostage," but simply says, "If you want it, we can make it a part of any deal package we create. Now that we know of something I can easily give to you, why don't we search for something that you can easily add to the deal? I'm sure if we discuss it a bit, we can find some item of value that may not mean too much to you but could really help me a lot."

Instead of the old stick-carrot-and-horse approach, where the dominant party holds one element of value like a bullwhip over the other's head, AVN suggests you use plain old-fashioned horse trading to identify throw-ins—elements of value that both parties can give to the other without much effort.

In many deals, you can identify certain options that serve interests for both sides and that don't cause any hardship or grief when they're tossed into the discussion. With surprising frequency, an offhand remark made in passing by one of the sides during the negotiation will often trigger the other party to say, "Hey! I could use that!"

In Escondido, California, the world-renowned Wild Animal Park is home to thousands of animals from all continents. This huge natural habitat is affiliated with the San Diego Zoo and boasts one of the best captive breeding programs in the world.

As you can imagine, this collection of untamed beasts goes through a prodigious amount of food each day. The end result of all that eating—the manure—causes quite a disposal headache for the park's zookeepers.

For years, disposal of the manure was quite a logistical problem. It had to be raked into piles, loaded into wheelbarrows, and dumped into trucks. The park would then pay a waste-disposal firm to remove the tons of droppings left by animals ranging in size from elephants to birds. The fees for this daily, weekly, monthly, and yearly service ran quite steep.

Finally, an enterprising private firm analyzed the problem and approached the park with a unique offer. Their company would take the animal waste and pay the park for the privilege. "What are you up to?" the park people surely asked. It turns out the firm planned to package the droppings as high-grade fertilizer for commercial farmers and growers.

Because the animals at the Wild Animal Park eat nothing but the best foods and feeds, their healthy digestive tracts turn out quality plant fertilizer. Negotiations quickly ended with the firm that was paid to haul the manure away and quickly began with the firm who paid to haul it away.

It's hard to categorize your perception of each of the elements of value in the deal. Because there are five of them (money, property, actions, rights, and risks) and they cover a diverse range of topics, it's not a one-size-fits-all approach. What may be extremely important to your side may not even have been considered by the other party, and because it's easy to get caught up in the heat of the negotiation, you or the other side can forget to mention certain value elements as you go along. Frank and open discussions can lead you both down a parallel path where you each say, "You need that? I can give you that!"

This trade-off approach is simple: Each time the other party discovers something he or she could use, you simply toss it into the collection of deal packages as one of the parts. The same goes for your side; you ask for a specific value item from them and you add it into the deal packages.

Whenever you give the other person something they want, just ask for something in return. This no-pressure approach is just like when you were a kid at the school lunch table, "I'll trade my apple for your orange and my chocolate pudding for your brownie."

You can delve into each of the five value elements—money, property, actions, rights, and risks—as deeply as you wish, depending upon the complexity of your deal. Because each category is typically very broadbased, you can get some good synergy going with the other party if you both brainstorm when, where, and how each element may fit into your deal. If the deal doesn't require such a significant level of detail, just make sure you touch on each value element mentally if not on paper.

Be careful not to rush past any of the value elements just to get down to the deal-packaging stage of the process. Some deals start out simply and end reasonably so; others start simply but, after careful analysis and discussion, reveal a whole host of other more complicated issues. Jumping from the discussion of interests and options to the creation of deal packages, without the necessary step of evaluating the various value elements in between, can cause you or the other party to lose value or overlook some very valuable possibilities.

Some power negotiators will want to gloss over the value elements that may not meet their needs or that they feel may distract you from accepting their good deal. One of the most recognizable negotiating tactics used by car salespeople involves bracketing the price. Instead of seeing money as just another of the five value elements, they want to lock you into a set price immediately. When they say, "How much would you like to pay per month?" instead of "Here is the best sticker price for this car," they can lock you into longer payment terms, higher interest rates, questionable financing tactics, and, ultimately, a higher sticker price for the car.

Starting the conversation with a quick discussion about money is not just common to the car sales industry; it's everywhere. Whether or not they will admit it freely, most people's perception of themselves revolves around their possession of money. Who has it, how much, where it comes from, and how to get more of it are all topics of interest, ranging from practiced nonchalance to an all-encompassing obsession and dozens of points in between for most people.

Let's face it: Most of your negotiations are going to deal with money, in some form or another. Unless they relate to personal matters or conflict resolutions, money is one of the main points of discussion in negotiations. Studies of marriage and family matters indicate the same thing; couples fight about money and children, in that order. Even if they don't have the latter, they're always interested in the state of flux surrounding the former.

Let's explore the five value elements in more detail. As you review each, keep in mind that they can work separately in some instances and together in others. Various combinations can become valuable to you in your deals, especially when they are mixed with the needs of the other party. Make sure you touch on each one as you discuss value options with the other parties. You or they may come up with something that you both might not have thought of before.

These five components that make up the option tree are the raw material from which you can construct possible deals.

Money: Not the Only Object

As popular rock singer Huey Lewis of "Huey Lewis and the News" so aptly puts it in one of his tunes, "If money is the root of all evil, I'd like to be a bad, bad man."

Most people want more of it, don't feel like they have enough of it to live comfortably, and fear they may lose it. Money is the root of power, influence, and position and people want to keep as much as possible. They don't want to part with more than a little of it, even if it doesn't physically belong to them, as in a business negotiation between one company and another. In short, much of what you see or do around a bargaining table will probably involve money. How you and the other party can keep or get enough to satisfy you both depends on the answers to a number of questions. Like no other value element, money is an intense issue:

Where will the money come from?

Who will provide it? When?

How will the money be divided between the two parties?

What physical form will the money take? What will "the money" look like? Cash? Credit? A check? Gold coins? A note payable? Stocks, bonds, or securities?

Who will hold it? Where?

How long will it last?

What are the associated costs with holding, saving, using, or transferring the money?

What about taxes on the money?

Let's suppose your American office is negotiating with a similar organization to undertake a joint venture in Australia. Your company will send a team of engineers to Melbourne to install one of your amazing new steam turbines. The Australian firm will send a team of its engineers to help you complete a proposal to make your steam turbines usable for a huge hydroelectric plant being built in the wilds of the Australian outback.

Money is one of the most important issues you'll both want to discuss. Who gets paid? When, how, and how much? Getting fair monetary value for your time, materials, and use of your personnel is a mutual concern for both of you, in addition to the main interest you both share—you want to supply their whole continent with steam turbines and they want to help you win the bid so they can operate the plant.

In this case, the money being exchanged is not a straight cash-for-cash deal, is it? Cash American and cash Australian aren't the same, thanks to a tiny detail known as the foreign currency exchange rate. The same situation can arise between any two firms in different countries.

If your firm is relatively cash-rich and you can afford to defer your monetary compensation in this deal for a short time, why not suggest that the Australian firm hold onto your fees? If interest rates (and the value of the Australian dollar) are high, let them take a small extra fee to manage your money in an interest-bearing account until exchange rates change so that both firms actually make more money in the deal.

If you decide to defer your payment, you'll need to consider who will manage the money, for how long, and where and how it will eventually be paid to you. Clearly, in this international deal, the exchange of money can take on some interesting sidelights.

Just how you set your fees for an international deal can make a tremendous difference in your compensation. What if you were involved in a business deal with a Japanese bank in Tokyo? Could you accept the equivalent amount of your fees in yen instead of your own currency? If it looks like there might be a long-term gain against the yen, would you be willing to defer your receipt of the money to gain more of it in the currency exchange? Might this be a better deal for both sides, because you might make more and they can save your fee for a short time and work with the money themselves?

These kinds of money trades are limited only by your imagination and the willingness of the other party to be amenable to your creativity, and these options can come as trade-offs for others in the deal.

The concept of trade-offs becomes important here again. If currency rates help your Australian or Japanese partners, what other elements of value might they be willing to give you for the opportunity to defer your payment? Could they offer you some collateral item that would enhance your business, improve your position in the marketplace, or lower your tax burdens? Could both parties entertain a variety of possible price points, each supported by a different set of trade-offs among the other value factors?

As our lives get more complicated and enriched by so many other factors, you can see that the typical price-only, cash-for-goods deals leave so much more to be desired. Money comes in so many different forms that it's a shame to classify a deal as cash-only unless that is absolutely all it really is.

Property: Visible and Invisible

While in most cases property refers to a physical entity, it could also involve intellectual properties like computer software, a magazine article, a copyright, a patent, a trademark, or something that is of both tangible and intangible value, like customer data base lists stored on a computer. Anything that resembles a capital asset can be classified as property.

If you wanted to buy the customer house list of your next largest competitor, the names would have a certain tangible and intangible value for you. You might be especially interested in how up-to-date the names are, what kind of buying power those listed have, or, better yet, what kind of buying potential they possess, and whether they will want to know more about your particular line of products or services.

If you were to make an offer to purchase this house list, you might want to build certain variations into the deal. If 50 percent of the names are up-to-date, accurate, and indicate buying interest, you might pay one fee for them. If the figure moves to 75 percent, you might pay another higher fee for them. This asset is multifaceted; it shares several attributes, including the ability to be resold to another interested company, rented to a mailing-list broker, or swapped with another firm. Like many deals, this piece of property has the elements of money tied all the way through it.

It's easier to fix an accurate price on a physical piece of property like a car, a house, a computer, or a bulldozer; it's more difficult to establish a monetary value of intellectual properties like the words that make up a training manual, a song, the lines of code in a software program, a copyright, or a patent for a new invention. You can see in these cases how the money element of value mixes in with the property element.

How do you put a monetary value on an intellectual property? It usually relates to its marketability. If you're novelist Stephen King and you come to the publisher with a new book idea, it may be entirely worth it to them to pay you $12 million for your next intellectual property. If you're writing a book about the biological structure of spiders, it may take just as much time and expertise for you to produce your book as it does Mr. King but will not be nearly as lucrative. The difference in your property and his lies in who will pay to read it.

When you discuss property as a value item with the other party, be flexible in your definitions and descriptions of what actually constitutes property. Physical presence is not the only criterion. Property can exist in the mind as well.

Actions: Who Does What

Actions are those things that people will do or won't do to carry out the final deal in a negotiation. For example, if you sell your furniture-making business to an associate, you may agree not to compete in the furniture-making business for at least five years. If you buy a large piece of factory equipment, the seller may agree to service the machine for free for a period of up to one year.

In most cases, you'll learn what the other party will do or won't do, or what is similarly expected of you by talking with them. Actions, as they relate to the AVN model, relate to movements or prohibitions: what you will do or refrain from doing for the other party or what they will do or refrain from. Some of these things will become clearer as the negotiation continues.

As you focus on the deal packages themselves, various action options become apparent, giving more structure to the final deal. You may agree to every request the other party makes or you may want to have a serious discussion about certain items. Conversely, the other party may have no problems agreeing to meet your needs concerning certain actions or not agree with any of them. The reasons for these wide ranges when it comes to actions often relates to the first value element—money. When you do or don't do something in the deal, it often affects the bottom line. No-compete clauses offer an example of this.

Rights: Who's Allowed to Do What

The unique difference between actions and rights lies in the stipulations: an action is something you're obligated to do and a right is something that you're entitled to do, whether or not you choose to do it.

The concept of rights, as in what you allow the other party to do or not do and what the other party allows you to do or not do doesn't just relate solely to business. Personal negotiations can also offer similar arrangements. Matters relating to family concerns, parent-teenager discussions, and marriage considerations also take the right-to-do under consideration. In business affairs, rights may relate to the use of names, copyrights, trademarks, patents, products, or services.

In real estate matters, easements or the right to travel across a certain parcel of land may be at issue during the negotiation. Water rights, gas, oil, and mineral rights, and other similar exploratory property rights may be at issue.

Professional sports teams often invoke certain rights as they pertain to players. These include the right to trade a player; talk with a player from another team; renegotiate a player's contract after a certain date; and the right to trade, waive, cut, or reassign a player.

This value element is limited only to the imaginations of the parties involved. You can grant the rights to almost any legal or moral activity, just as you can prohibit access to nearly any activity. Giving the rights to get access to a person, place, or thing can range from easy to extremely difficult, because the fair value of that item is usually at stake.

Risks: Who Takes the Heat

Of all five value elements, the concept of risks (which ones you'll take and which ones the other party will take) sometimes offers the best chance to really get creative. In any negotiation, you can assume all of the risk in the deal, split it in equal portions with the other party, have the other party take on all of the risks, or come to an agreement anywhere between these three choices. How much you or the other party takes on often depends on the level of trust and empathy between you.

High empathy and high trust mean more willingness to assume risks or at least share them. Low empathy and low trust mean the other party (or you) will feel less inclined to take on the risks. If you don't trust someone, you certainly won't feel like giving him or her the chance to put you in a greater position of risk.

The added value negotiating model is built upon the concept of providing the greater good. There is little chance you will share or assume great risk to the person who tries to manipulate you in a negotiating session.

In business deals, the assumption of risk often relates to money, as in who will pay for any losses, loan the money, get the funds, hold the assets, and so on. Whenever you have a new venture such as a joint deal between two entrepreneurs, a merger between two like-minded firms, a leveraged buyout (LBO), or a similar takeover plan, there is always a notable amount of risk with the financial side.

Buying a car from your local Honda dealer involves a certain amount of risk for both buyer and seller; but it's usually well-protected on both sides by rules, safety checks (like a credit report), or past practices (like a referral from a satisfied friend or the fact that the dealer has been in business for many years).

Buying a large company generates tremendous amounts of risk. Whereas the car dealer and the car buyer are willing to share the risk equally, in these kinds of big deals, it becomes necessary for the health and safety of the deal for all parties to share various aspects of risk to ensure that the deal will work.

To use a practical example, the purchase of life insurance carries an assumption of risk on both sides. The insurance company is betting you won't die and in effect you're betting you will. The premiums you pay into a typical term life policy are certainly not equivalent to the value of the insurance policy amount. If, for example, you purchased $200,000 worth of term life insurance and locked in your premiums, you could pay $350 per year for the next 20 years. The total you pay would hardly reach the equivalent cash amount of the value of the policy.

So how does the insurance company make money? They reinvest your premiums and make their money with your money. They're gambling on the chance that you'll outlive your money and in essence they win. If you die earlier than their life expectancy tables predict, then they lose and, as hard as it seems to imagine, you win.

Who carries how much risk becomes an important part of any deal package you put together. How the risk is apportioned between the two parties should be clear in any group of deal packages you create. In fact, you can even pay a third party to assume certain risks, such as by purchasing a commercial insurance policy covering some aspects of the deal.

None of the five value elements—money, property, actions, rights, and risks—is mutually exclusive of the others. In its own way, each can make up a large or small part of any deal package you create. The key to understanding each of these value elements lies in your ability to think creatively, make a careful inventory of the value that is potentially available in any deal, look hard into the future, and balance your interests with those of the other party.

DRAWING THE OPTION TREE

Some people, who tend to be a bit more analytical and methodical thinkers than most, feel more comfortable if they can write down everything important that is said during a negotiation. They can relax a bit more if they're able to capture their thoughts on paper. This process also helps them organize their ideas in a cohesive manner and keep track of what the other party says and wants.

If you're the type who likes to "wing it" and keep track of everything in your head, you might want to change your negotiating practices to be a bit more like the methodical, write-it-all-down types. The benefits far outweigh any inconvenience you may feel.

Many bulldogs and foxes operate on the principle, "If it's not on paper, I didn't agree to it." Their frame of reference is to operate as though they don't like to write things down because they fear that the items on paper might become too permanent. If you encounter this kind of behavior, where the other party says, "Oh, don't worry about that. We'll remember to fill in all the little details later," be prepared to deal with a crafty operator.

All of those seemingly little details are actually the crux of your negotiation. Leaving the interests and the elements of value to later memory is a good way to set things up for misunderstandings.

Writing things down allows you to create a reasonably clear inventory of what you've discussed. It protects both of you now and later. Many hard feelings can arise if one side says one thing and the other side completely disagrees. With no hard copy to establish who said what to whom, what was once a good negotiating process can turn sour.

Using the option tree pen-and-paper model can help you identify and organize the five elements of value (money, property, actions, rights, and risks) much better than if you just relied on your memory or, worse, on the memory of the other person.

Just like the window of interest, the option tree is a model built on simplicity and ease of use. You just make a list of the five value elements across a sheet of paper and then list the various options and suboptions you discover below the main categories.

FIGURE 5-1
Using the Option Tree—Example

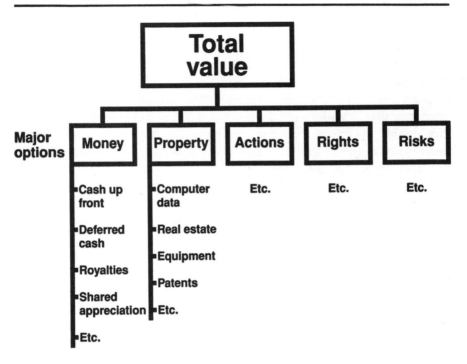

Options lead to other suboptions, which can lead to even more sub-options, until you've filled an entire page with ideas, as illustrated in Figure 5–1.

An even easier way to draw the option tree is to use a technique called brain-mapping. To use this method, start with a clean sheet of paper and write one of the value elements right smack in the center of the page. From there, draw lines that radiate from the center, attaching a word, phrase, or key piece of information to each line. Each time you come up with a new piece of information, start a new line or add it to an existing line. Some people call these spider diagrams because they look like webs. It's called a brain map because the ideas look like cities and the lines look roads, such as in Figure 5–2.

Drawing the option tree in this manner is good if you have a lot of information to organize. If the negotiating subject is especially complex or the value items demand a lot of work, use the brain map to draw a

FIGURE 5–2
Using the "Brain Map" as a Technique for Drawing Option Trees

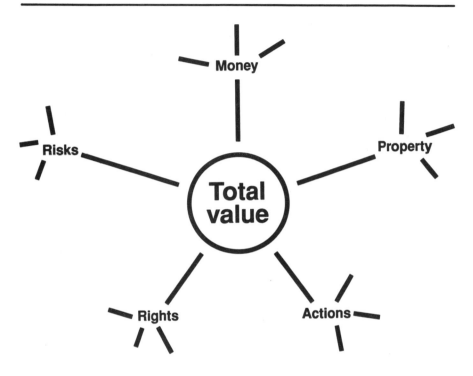

more complete option tree. No matter how you choose to draw your respective option tree, don't make it more complex than it is. Choose an approach that is easy for you and will help you and the other party keep track of what was said and done.

For any large-scale project where there are a number of moving parts, deadlines, high-money figures, and the like, your approach to the negotiating situation justifies the kind of energy, activity, research, and discussion that the models of the added value negotiating method provide. Don't rely on luck or memory to get what you want; use the steps in the method to keep track of everything. It's always better to have too much paper than not enough.

By now you can see that if you plan to use the AVN method for a large negotiating task, it will take some work to get it done. Added value negotiating is a hands-on, research-based model that demands effort and commitment.

It's not a shoot-from-the-hip, gunfighter method where you can breeze into the room, make a few pithy suggestions, and get the deal done correctly. Creating deal packages for further review and study will take some effort, but the process itself can make any deal you choose better than if you hadn't used it at all.

As with most things in life, the harder you work the better deal you get. Coming to the negotiating table ready to use models like the window of interest and the option tree can put you far ahead of the traditional method, before you even start. By modeling the assertive and fair behavior that is so much a part of added value negotiating, you can help them feel comfortable with letting you guide the negotiations by using this methodical approach.

TRADE-OFFS: CREATIVE WAYS TO ADD VALUE TO THE DEAL

As previously mentioned, interests and options are not the same things. They may seem similar and people may confuse the two because they don't remain focused. In any negotiation that is the chance for the other party to leave with a better deal.

Too many would-be dealmakers focus all of their attentions on some one element of value in the deal; not surprisingly, it's money. By putting all of their eggs into the money basket, they fail to see or even look for other nonmonetary ways to make a good deal better.

Suppose the other party starts off the negotiation by saying, "I want $200,000 for my house, take it leave it." If you're smart, you're either going to have to leave it, or ask them if they plan to actually negotiate. Asking for one firm price and refusing to discuss any other deal is not a negotiation, because you don't have any opportunity to make another offer.

The win-lose teachers instruct their pupils to first figure out the happy medium between the last-resort price (what you'll take if you get desperate) and the not-a-chance price (what you're sure the other party just won't pay). "Find this price and stick to it come hell or high water," they counsel. "Make them come up to you, don't go down to them."

One negotiating expert advises having a concession strategy, which is a sequence of levels you should go through in your demands, on the way to your final position. These might be, for example, a series of price points. "Of course," he counsels, "you should try to make as few concessions as possible, and shoot for the best level you can get."

This not-so-helpful advice causes many of the problems that surround most negotiations. It's tactics like these that make people feel uncomfortable and unwilling to make deals that are good for everyone. When faced with a no-win situation, many people simply cut their losses, accept the best deal they can, and get out quickly. The end result is that both sides leave feeling like they probably could have got a better deal had they negotiated with someone else.

When faced with a take-it-or-leave-it price, the added value negotiator says, "That's an interesting figure. I'd be happy to talk with you about why that figure means so much to you. Money is certainly important, but we can also talk about some of the other elements of value that are apparent while we search for a good deal."

The mutual search for value forces you to improve the way you think and communicate with the other party. The AVN method asks you to extend beyond the obvious and look for the hidden value; it exists in every deal, it's just a matter of locating it.

Can you and the other party both put on your thinking caps and find some more things to add to the deal that you both may have missed earlier? Can you say, "Now that the negotiation is in the option stage, can we look harder and add something that may make it even better? Are we overlooking some ways of creating value that would help both of us?"

If you can't have this kind of discussion with the other party, maybe because they're far too secretive or hostile, then you'll need to carry on the conversation with yourself. Remember, AVN is not a give-away method of negotiating. As much as you may believe in fairness and a good deal for everyone involved, you needn't place your interests second. If you can rise above the mind-set of bargaining and focus on meeting needs and identifying options that met those needs, then you can come out well, no matter how poorly the other side negotiates.

The concept of trade-offs makes AVN unique as a negotiating method. In any true deal (not extortive win-lose no-good-deal charades) you certainly will have things the other party wants and vice versa. Establishing what those items are, the value they represent, and what each of you will do or give up to get them is the key to mutual success.

Let's look at a few examples where trading one or more of the five value elements can add more to any deal. As you review these scenarios,

think of even more ways you yourself would add value if you were involved in the search for a fair deal.

Suppose that you are in the process of buying a house. The seller has
told you he wants $180,000 for his house. It's only 10 years old, in a
good neighborhood, and has a nice swimming pool in the backyard. You
know from research that similar houses are going for $140,000 to
$190,000, depending on the number of rooms, extra amenities, and the
location. Before countering his price with your own, you explain the
added value negotiating process and suggest you both look for elements
of value you both share. In the course of the discussion, the seller men-
tions that he and his wife are moving across town to a new house. It's a
nice place, but it lacks a swimming pool. The seller is not a big swimming pool fan but his wife teaches children's swimming lessons throughout the summer. Up until now, she had used their home swimming pool
to teach the children and the extra income was substantial.

It's clear from your conversation that one of the seller's interests not
really related to the sale of his house is additional income for his family.
What options might you suggest to help him serve this interest?

- Why not extend the escrow period from the standard 30 days to
  60 or even 90 days? Let his wife finish out the summer by continuing to teach swimming lessons from their home pool. In return for
  this right to use the pool, you could make a lower offer on the sales
  price of the house.
- Why not allow his wife to use the swimming pool during the times
  when you and your spouse are at work? She could teach her lessons
  on weekdays between 10:00 A.M. and 2:00 P.M. without disturbing
  you. In exchange for this right, you could shorten the escrow period
  to better meet your move-in needs.
- If you're having trouble coming up with the down payment or
  qualifying for the entire loan amount, why not work out a shared
  equity deal where you move in, take over his mortgage payments
  plus an extra amount paid to him each month, and sign a balloon
  payment note payable in five years for the balance of the loan? His
  wife could continue to teach swimming, he would get some extra
  rental income, and you would earn a small interest in the property
  until you could fully afford to buy it.

Suppose that you are involved in a business merger. You own a luxury
soap company and another party owns a premium towel company. You've
decided to join forces and market your products together in the same

package. He has a warehouse full of towels; he buys his stock from a foreign manufacturer. You have a soap plant nearby that produces thousands of bars an hour. He wants to start a small towel-making operation inside his warehouse, offering a better quality towel and lowering his importing costs. You want to get your soap into more prestigious markets to which he already has access with his towels. With the five value elements in mind, what options might you both offer to serve your mutual interests in the venture?

- Your soap company is right on the railroad line. Why not offer to store an inventory of towels, so you can package and ship the end product by using your box car? In exchange for this, the towel company could introduce you to his best distributors.
- Why not offer to help pay for the towel-making machines? With your added investment, you can get a little better deal on the end product, like a higher product mark-up for the use of your capital.
- Your new soap-and-towel venture will require more employees to run both operations. Why not have both of you to agree to cross-train your respective employees in the ways of making and packaging both soap and towels? A group of these trained people could trade off and work at both plants over the course of the year.

Suppose that you are negotiating a raise. You've worked hard for this organization for two years and you feel your good work qualifies you for a healthy raise. You do the job of several people and everyone is always telling you how valuable you are. When you approach your boss about it, she tells you how these tough economic times have really tied her hands. She does agree to sit down with you to discuss your interests. You propose the following options to meet your interests:

- What kind of nonmonetary benefits can she offer you? How about more vacation time? This way you can afford to take a few days off to work on your part-time home product sales business.
- What if she changes your job title to reflect your wide range of duties? Maybe she can exchange this job title for a raise by making it a nonmonetary promotion. Perhaps a more prestigious job title would help you build your resume should you ever change divisions in the firm or leave the company completely.
- Perhaps she can offer to defer your raise until the start of the next fiscal year or until the start of the next budget period. She could guarantee the pay increase in writing to take place at a more fiscally convenient time for the company.

Each of these cases highlights a simple but powerful feature of the added value negotiating approach, that is, the use of trade-offs. One side asks for something he or she needs and then offers something in return, or one party discovers an interest and then tries to satisfy it by horse-trading back and forth until both parties are happy with what they receive.

Keep in mind that this trading of options to satisfy interests can take place during any kind of negotiation, not just typical business deals involving money and other exchanges of monetary value for goods or services. This give-and-take method can take much of the disharmony out of relationship deals and help you to resolve personal conflicts between yourself or other people.

If you were to take part in any of these deals listed above, you would start by making a list of the interests on both sides—you would create the window of interest. Then you would identify the options available to satisfy those interests—you would draw the option tree. From there, it's just an easy jump to the process of creating alternative deal packages, which the next chapter will discuss in detail.

Chapter Six

Creating Deal Packages
Never Make Just One Offer

"And yet, as a businessman, I can't help but feel a grudging admiration."

So far, you've clarified the interests of all parties, to their satisfaction, and you've identified the options for fulfilling those interests by means of the various elements of value available. You have skillfully used the window of interest and the option tree, and now you're ready for step three of the AVN process, i.e., actually designing various deal packages for consideration by the parties involved.

The reasoning behind the multiple-deals feature of the AVN method is simple yet powerful: Most people feel more comfortable choosing from several alternatives than having to react to a single offer. Rejecting the only deal on the table brings everything to a grinding halt, but rejecting any of several deal packages feels more like a decision than an act of aggression. People feel more empowered because they have been given the opportunity to choose rather than reject or accept.

If they don't like any of the deal packages put before them, they can always say that they don't and explain why. Even if this happens (it rarely does because of all the communication that goes on during the development of the deal packages themselves), the conglomeration of unacceptable deal packages may contain the elements of new and more appealing deals.

Letting people choose from a number of deals can also give you insight into what they think is valuable. It tests their responses to different types of value. When they choose one deal from a collection, you can ask yourself, "To what are they responding? Which element of value in that deal appeals to them and why?" You can be sure these questions are being asked and answered in their own minds as well.

Further, it's almost built into our human nature to reject the first thing we're offered. Our personal history negotiating tells us not to take the first offer and to always try to whittle the other person down. Added value negotiating and the existence of more than one deal stops this offer-counteroffer process in its tracks.

A group of deal packages can also serve as a buffer between you and the bulldog or the fox. With so many choices, it's more difficult for them to gain much footing and center their attacks on a single deal. It tends to seduce them into a focus on value instead of a focus on persuasion.

LETTING STRUCTURE NEGOTIATE FOR YOU

Another name for added value negotiating could easily be structured negotiating. The real purpose of the method is to displace the interpersonal tension, pressure, and anxiety to a process people feel they can trust. It helps them approach the subject of negotiation as a step-by-step method to follow, rather than a battle of wits they must engage in with the other side. It takes the sudden-death fear out of negotiating and removes much of the apprehension about being taken because the process itself conveys a certain assurance that it will lead to acceptable results for all concerned.

Following the method helps both people to stay in their comfort zones. Of course, there is always a certain amount of stress that surrounds any significant negotiation and in most instances this edge to the environment is healthy; it tends to make you stay on your toes and not walk into the deal like a lamb headed for the back of the butcher's shop. A little tension almost always helps us perform better. Test-takers, professional and Olympic athletes, and emergency services personnel will all admit that a small dose of adrenaline makes them more effective.

Of course, on the other extreme, too much stress and tension can make you completely ineffective. If you're overstressed, you'll be more likely to freeze, make an ill-timed decision, or otherwise act rashly or out of character. The key is to strike a balance and find the happy medium between a lackadaisical approach and a fear-struck one.

Following the structure of the AVN method, completing the steps, and documenting your efforts with the two pen-and-paper models can give you the inner confidence and self-assurance you need to get through even the most demanding negotiations.

By the time you're ready to start constructing a set of deal packages, as this chapter will explain, you will want to have done a lot of preparation and research. If the negotiation is significant and you have used the AVN method to its fullest, you'll be in a much better position to create the best deal for all parties. This position of confidence can keep you, and ultimately the other party, in a comfort zone environment.

NEGOTIATING FROM THE TOTAL PICTURE

A critical advantage of the AVN method is that it starts with and stays with the total picture of the negotiation. This tends to neutralize a number of the power tricks used by aggressive negotiators. For example, one of the favorite tricks of bulldogs in particular is the so-called *salami* technique. Instead of looking at the entire situation as a whole, the salami maker will say, "Let's settle the issue of *x* first." Then he or she will proceed to take one item of the negotiation (the money issue, for example) and drive for a settlement on that one topic.

The problem with this one-piece-at-a-time approach is that it may put you at a significant disadvantage later. Should you try to bring up issue *x* at a later time, he or she will counter you with, "Oh, no you don't! That matter has already been settled! We agreed to that figure, time, condition, etc., minutes, hours, or days ago. You can't go back on that now!"

One of the best ways to stay out of this and similar standoffs, where one party tries to pick and choose and battle for each individual item, is to make the boundaries clear at the beginning of any meeting. This conversation with the other party should set the stage for the rest of the encounter.

You can start by saying, "I have a certain way I like to approach negotiating. I make my mind up in advance what the whole range of the deal is. I want to get a sense of what value is in any deal we create together. I'm not willing to settle any issue in isolation from the other elements of value."

The other party may counter with the standard response that says, "Never mind all of that. Let's just settle on issue *x* first."

That may be fine with the other person, but it shouldn't sit too well with you. His or her issue *x* could be any of a number of things, ranging from price, terms, quantities, dates, actions, etc., but what it usually signifies, at least in the context of these early stages of the negotiation, is a position that allows him or her to set the stage for his or her own agenda. The other person wants to settle one piece of the deal first and then once that item has been settled, he or she will continue to the next targeted issue.

If the other party says, flatly, "Here's my deal. Take it or leave it," you should be in a position to say, "Thanks. I'll leave it. When someone tries to force me to take a deal I don't want, I don't. That's not the way I do business." If you have to accept an offer at gunpoint like this, then you probably don't have much of a negotiation to begin with.

There is a certain assertive, calm, and noncombative stance to the AVN method. Added value negotiating is an approach that requires its users to have a certain amount of vision. It works for the best when you can see beyond the proposal in front of you, especially if it has been shoved at you by the other side like junk mail through your office door. The vision you'll require calls for you to take a helicopter view of the entire negotiation. Instead of wasting time by focusing on insignificant or distracting issues, use the big picture view of the entire situation as your backdrop for the search for value.

When you can put aside distracting elements like emotions, personality differences, and other related pressures, you can get a better overall idea of what you want, what the other party wants, and what might be good for both of you.

CREATING ALTERNATIVE DEAL PACKAGES

The attempt in creating a group of deal packages is to maximize the value involved for all parties while giving them choices. The source material for the deal packages is the whole range of elements of value that you have inventoried either alone or with the other person.

What the phrase *added value* really means is that by designing deal packages effectively, you can put together (or add) elements of value that both people never imagined could be part of any deal when they began. Your use of deal packages helps to add an element of psychological victory to the search for a good deal. They may find themselves saying, "You know, I never thought this kind of deal was even possible. I would have been happy to take half of this deal. Now I'm getting much more. What started out as a deal over issue *x* has become issue *x* plus so much more."

All of this extends the value of the final deal far beyond what either side had anticipated. The synergistic effect of clarifying the interests together, identifying the options together, and designing the deal packages together builds the level of empathy. When the other side feels comfortable with the process, he or she may think, "I'm already getting more than I expected. I don't feel like splitting hairs over some of the smaller stuff because the deal I've chosen is so much better than I thought was first possible."

The physical process of creating the deal packages is easy. You (or whoever plans to create the deals) take a piece of paper and divide it into four or five squares. Reviewing the window of interest and the option tree, you assemble a number of deals that bring together the elements that are important. Let your instincts be your guide and make sure you balance the interests that are important to both parties.

This is where the whole issue of generosity comes into play. How much you give to the other party, or how much the other party gives you if he or she is creating the deals, depends on the levels of empathy, trust, and cooperation you feel between you. In some cases, like with chronic bulldogs, they may be quite low, in which case you'll have to use greater caution when designing feasible deal packages that will account for your interests. In other instances, the levels will be so high that you won't mind making certain arrangements that add more to the deal for them than for you. The concept of trade-offs becomes important here. If you add something to all deal packages that helps your position, be ready to add something else that helps the other side too.

If you can sit at the table elbow to elbow rather than face-to-face in the spirit of a mutual search for a good deal, it becomes easier to play with the various options and to make a good deal for all of you.

Here are some guidelines to consider as you design your deal packages:

- Review the window of interest and the option tree carefully; make additions or corrections as necessary.
- Use the Chinese-menu approach, that is, select options from each category, so that each deal includes options in each of the five elements of value—money, property, actions, rights, and risks.
- Diversify the deals by emphasizing a different balance of factors in each one. Make each deal interesting in its own unique way.
- Design deal packages—various combinations of the value elements—that seem to balance the interests of all parties.
- Recognize that each deal is a different way to balance interests, through a different arrangement of the value elements.

If you recall the previous discussion on setting constraints and ground rules, you can use those guideposts to focus the design of deal packages. If when trying to create three or four deal packages for a large-scale purchase it becomes clear that outside financing is not only acceptable but is also absolutely necessary to the success of any deal, then the choice to finance the deal by yourselves is just not an option. Any deal package you or the other party creates must include the decision to look outside for financial assistance. Creating deal packages that don't account for the real-life constraints is just a waste of time. Focus your efforts on making deal packages that are actually feasible as well as appealing to both sides.

You can certainly ask the seller of the house you want to throw in two plane tickets to Maui as an incentive. If he agrees to this provision, good for you. If not, don't waste time by trying to get it included as a member of several deal packages.

The examples that follow this kind of parameter-setting are infinite. By understanding the respective interests and the options for meeting them, you or the other party can look at the window of interest and the option tree and say, "Now that we know everything we can in terms of what we both want, let's see if we can pull out some common areas and use those as the basis for several deals."

The boundaries of any deal can serve as a filter for both sides. If the other side says, "I will not consider any deal that has this, this, and this in it," then you've discovered areas that shouldn't go into the deal packages you make. Of course, if you want to see those particular elements in your deals, then you may have to go back to the beginning of the AVN process and find out why it's so important those items are omitted from the other party's deal.

Because the dealmaking phase of the AVN process is so flexible, one or both parties can say, "As I look at all of the interests and options on my side, I would prefer that we create deals that are heavy in issues x and y. Issue z doesn't mean that much to me, but I can live with it if it's important to you. But I really would like to see more emphasis placed on x and y, at least for my own benefit. I'd be happy to talk about it with you or we can just put those issues into all deals right now."

Keep in mind that the creation process of any deal is not regimented to any one person or the other. One party can defer to the other and let him or her come up with several deals; both parties can work separately from each other and compare feasible deals later, as is helpful with large deals, with those involving many people, or with two distinct entitities like merging corporations.

Two parties can ask a third party to come up with some deal packages for them or you could be asked to review the interests and options for two parties and act as a third party for them by creating deal packages based on your understanding of their needs. This last option is helpful during conflict-resolution situations or negotiations where both sides want to look to a disinterested outsider to help them settle their differences.

If you feel comfortable with the other side, you can ask them to propose some deals but, for maximum benefit for both parties, why not suggest that you create the deals for both of you? The more experienced AVN negotiator can usually develop deals that show an extra measure of creative added value.

No matter what happens, you still have the right to say no to any deal on the table. You can exercise your veto power over any of them, even at this late stage in the negotiation. With so many packages to choose from, you can almost always find one that you like. If the other party ever objects to any deal package, you can always fall back to the window of interest and the option tree and say "Here's what we discussed. Here are some of the things we both agreed are important. Here's the rationale for why they appear in these deal packages."

The deal package creation process can let you freewheel a bit. Using your creativity, your intuition, and your built-in barometer of the mood and spirit of the other party, you can be a little outrageous. Why not suggest something totally out of the ordinary and see if it appeals to them? It never hurts to ask and the worst that can happen is he or she will exercise a little veto power and say "no."

Creating deal packages can take 15 minutes, 15 days, or even 15 months, depending upon the complexity of the subject, the size and availability of both parties, and where each side is in the meet-and-confer cycle. It can take place on the first day of the negotiation or the hundredth. The process is not restricted to deadlines, other than those created by the needs of the participants. If you need to come to a deal now, then you'll obviously work much faster than if there were no fixed deadline.

However long it takes to come up with your deal packages, don't be in a hurry to put any old thing on paper. What you create is subject to interpretation and acceptance by the other party. Rushing through this part of the AVN process because you want to conclude the negotiation is not wise. Don't make critical mistakes this late in the game. You need to ask yourself if you can live with each deal you create; obviously you will like some more than others, but it's important not to rush through this critical stage. You won't be able to go back and easily make corrections later as you can now. Work out the numbers, do the calculations, and make sure the deals you create really meet your interests effectively.

USING RESEARCH AND ANALYSIS: WHAT'S A DEAL WORTH?

When you were in school, you probably didn't like doing schoolwork too much, unless it involved a subject you truly enjoyed. Each of your teachers always told you how important their respective subject was and how you would use these newly learned skills later in life. It was often difficult to see the lifelong value of knowing the capital of Iceland, the gross national product of Burma, or the Pythagorean theorem.

The concept of doing your homework has changed a bit now that you're an adult. The issues you face now have grown in size and stature to a position of more prominence. You may have to negotiate deals that involve millions, that affect hundreds or even thousands of people, or you may have to make a deal that improves something important for just you or your family. Whatever the case, doing your negotiating homework takes on a heightened significance. The bottom line to you should always be: "What are any of these deals worth to me? Right now? In the future?" If you don't know the answers to these questions before you choose an acceptable deal, how can you know that you got the best deal possible?

The amount of homework you'll have to do to put together deal packages usually relates to the complexity of the negotiation. Complicated issues demand more work; simple deals can take shape on a single piece of paper. How you work depends on what you want out of the deal and how much pressure is on you. No matter how much information you need to compile, it will take some discipline on your part to find out what you need to know and not to rely on guesswork or spurious sources of advice or information.

If you're the lead negotiator for a large business negotiation and your boss is counting on you to make the best deal possible for your company, chances are good that you'll be spending nights and weekends chained to your desk, eating vending machine food, and searching for every interest and element of value on both sides of the table.

You may need to create spreadsheets; or study cost analyses; marketing forecasts; production reports; financial reports; pie charts; graphs; charts; maps; refer to legal, medical, or scientific books; or weed through a host of other complicated, time-demanding, and extensive business literature. You might have to talk with other people inside or outside your organization, make telephone calls, write letters, request reports, or even travel to other cities, companies, or factories to gather material. Hard work now will help you in spades later, both in your initial meetings with the other side and especially during the deal-package creation process.

It may help for you to see research and information gathering as your own security blanket. The more you know, the better you'll be able to make accurate decisions. Likewise, the more you know going into the negotiation, the better you'll be able to make good decisions under the potential stress and strain.

As an example, let's say a company comes to you with an offer to take your product outside the United States and be the sole overseas distributor. They make you an offer based on their understanding of your costs, markups, distributions, etc. It looks pretty good on paper, but how can you tell if it's worth accepting? Research, research, research.

What kind of gross revenues are they talking about? What kind of margins are involved? Will you have any increased manufacturing, inventory, or delivery costs? Have they provided you answers to these questions or will you need to find them yourself?

You might start by calling an associate in another industry who has a similar overseas deal worked out with another firm. Tell your friend about the deal that has been handed to you and ask if the numbers make sense and sound fair. He or she may tell you the deal is a generous one and to accept it wholeheartedly. Then again, he or she may tell you the figures are way off the mark and even border on being grossly unfair for your industry.

You could also sit down with your production and distribution managers and show them the figures. You might want to read some trade journals that offer overseas product sales numbers, call the Commerce Department for some help, or even go back to the other party and ask him or her for some actual figures from similar deals.

There are two important questions here: "What is this worth to us?" and "What is it worth to the other party?" If you can answer these two questions with information backed by research, not just by hazy guesses or blanket assurances from the other side, then you're in a better position to say yes or no to their deal. Don't underestimate the value of doing some hard pencil-and-paper work to discover the answers to questions you may have. The time to know something is before it becomes a deal-breaking issue. Research can keep you from making mistakes about the value involved.

And, of course, don't overlook the possibility that information provided by the other party could be inaccurate, misleading, or downright dishonest. In some situations, dishonesty is almost a norm. And in all situations, it's just good business to verify all of the data involved.

For example, you might be thinking of buying a small business from its current owner. It's only reasonable to ask for an audited financial statement or for the recent tax returns for the business, rather than accept the owner's claims about the revenues and costs.

Just as added value negotiating must be assertive as well as generous, it must also be realistic as well as open and transparent.

Chapter Seven

Balancing Interests
Choosing the Best Deal

Ashleigh Brilliant, © Brilliant Enterprises, 1974.

At this point, you are probably comfortable with the idea of offering the other side optional deal packages to choose from, rather than one proposal that they must counterpropose against. In the previous chapter we explored the experience of deal-building, that is, designing alternative deal packages that can meet all interests. Now it's time to begin converging on one or more deal packages that can become the basis for the final agreement.

Step 4 of the AVN method will help you take the assortment of deal packages you've designed and evaluate them. This calls for doing your own appraisal carefully and for meeting with the other side to discuss openly the relative merits of each package.

MEETING IN THE SPIRIT OF COOPERATION

Recalling that the basic meet-and-confer cycle is a recurring process for reinforcing empathy and exchanging useful information, we can now use it to guide us to a successful deal. We can get together with the other party and test for consensus.

At this point in the AVN process, it's important to assess the state of empathy and mutuality of purpose that exists between the parties involved. This is usually just a common-sense judgment, although there can sometimes be a bit of uncertainty. Ask yourself some simple questions:

- How are we feeling, personally, toward the other party?
- What impressions are we getting from them that show how they're feeling toward us?
- Are the lines of communication open? Do we return each other's telephone calls and faxes? Do we voluntarily share information? Do we answer each other's questions?
- If there are difficult points involved in the negotiation, do we talk openly and frankly about them? If misunderstandings or possible negative feelings arise, are we able to bring them up and work through them? Are we developing a pattern of getting along well with each other?
- Are both sides acting and talking like there will be a deal? Are we talking like colleagues and business associates or like representatives of our two sides? Is there a movement and a momentum toward consensus?

If there is a problem with empathy at this point, there will probably be a problem with consensus. If you're getting the impression the other party is reluctant to talk, seems inclined to withhold information, and seems to be responding from a role rather than from positive feelings toward you, you might as well deal with it sooner rather than later. You need to get an accurate fix on the situation, see whether your hunches are correct, and, if there is an empathy problem, you need to discover what's causing it and go to work to correct it.

An empathy problem is not usually a problem arising in and of itself, but rather a reflection of what's been going on between the parties up to some point. Primary empathy problems can arise because of the basic difficulties in dealing with the issues or because of someone's less-than-cooperative negotiating style. Secondary empathy problems can result from factors unrelated to the exchange of value, such as stress and fatigue, simple misunderstandings and communications mix-ups, personality quirks, or temporary setbacks due to changing circumstances.

What you have to do to solve the empathy problem and restore feelings of cooperation and collaboration will depend on the kind of problem you're having and what's causing it.

Every meeting or conversation with the other party gives you another chance to check on the empathy level and to head off problems that might be developing. This is why it is important to make each meeting as open, candid, cordial, and cooperative as possible. As you plan for any get-together with the other party, remind yourself of the empathy builders and empathy killers that can affect the outcome of the meeting.

Empathy killers

1. Putting stress on either party with the logistics of the meeting (e.g., choosing an inconvenient location, a difficult time of day, or an uncomfortable meeting environment that doesn't support the free exchange of ideas; not providing time for rest after travel or to prepare adequately).

2. Imposing excessive formality on the proceedings (e.g., prescribing seating arrangements that put two parties on opposite sides of the table or the room, wearing formal business attire, using formal titles to refer to the leaders of the parties involved, or presenting an overly formal agenda with formal presentations of factual material).

3. Limiting opportunities for people to interact on a personal basis (e.g., scheduling short, business-only meetings with both sides departing immediately or allowing other business matters to cut the meeting short or interfere with it).

4. Yielding to personalities and social styles of the people in the meeting (i.e., allowing only the technical experts to control the agenda, without consideration of the social or interpersonal factors that enrich the relationship-building process).

5. Adding inappropriate pressure or urgency to settle issues to reach consensus (e.g., discouraging adequate discussion of critical topics, forcing issues to a close with inadequate information, or forcing consensus rather than exploring the interests and feelings of all parties).

Empathy builders tend to be just the reverse of empathy killers. They are the things you can do to help people feel comfortable, keep them in their comfort zones, and support the ongoing development of the relationship. Here are some empathy builders you might want to consider in your meetings.

Empathy builders

1. Tending to the creature needs and comfort of the others (e.g., meeting them personally at the airport and escorting them to their hotel for a rest, starting the meeting at a convenient and comfortable time, allowing breaks, serving food and refreshments that build energy rather than sap it, and using a meeting environment that encourages the comfortable exchange of ideas).

2. Keeping the level of formality appropriate to the needs of the situation (e.g., encouraging casual dress if possible, getting on a first-name basis if the cultural considerations support it, sharing views and feelings early in the discussion to help each party get familiar with the other, and using humor to put people in a friendly and creative frame of mind).

3. Building a social or interpersonal basis for the relationship if appropriate (e.g., setting aside time for relaxation, entertainment, a bit of recreation, or perhaps a quick guided tour of the host city).

4. Running the meeting with a style and agenda that enables all parties to express their views, interests, and feelings (e.g., keeping the format flexible and changeable as needed, sharing information freely, having resources at hand to process information and make copies, and giving all parties a voice in what gets discussed and how).

5. Considering and developing all important issues (e.g., encouraging factual support, open discussion, a pace that achieves consensus quickly without steamrolling those who may disagree or need more discussion; testing consensus carefully; and clarifying areas of agreement and dissent).

There is ample evidence that negotiators who pay close attention to the development of empathy between the parties involved make it easier to deal with the various questions and concerns involved in the search for a deal. Empathy puts people in a more open, cooperative, and accommodating mood. Further, it tends to make most people more trusting and more generous, in the sense that they are more likely to offer value cooperatively than they might if they were feeling uneasy and defensive.

As a result, a habit of checking the empathy level and nurturing it has a double payoff. First, it helps you go further and faster in building deals that involve real value for all parties. Second, it just helps everybody feel better about the whole project, and that's a worthwhile benefit all by itself.

EVALUATING AND COMPARING THE DEALS

We can all agree that just having everyone feeling happy and empathetic is not, in and of itself, enough to guarantee an effective outcome. We have to invoke some rational and reasonably objective process for assessing the relative value offered to the various parties by the various deal packages and use this process as a basis for closing in on one arrangement agreed to by all parties. Now we move from the divergent phase to the convergent phase.

Evaluating deal packages can, of course, range from a very simple and intuitive process all the way to a very sophisticated analytical one, depending on the magnitude and complexity of the negotiation. At the small-and-simple end of the spectrum it's often a matter of having each side look at the three, four, or five variations they've designed and choose the one that's most inviting. If all parties find the same arrangement most inviting, then the analysis phase is basically done.

Other situations will be more complicated and will merit a more thoughtful analysis. One convenient method, and still a relatively simple one, is to ask each of the parties in the negotiation to evaluate the various deal packages on a simple yes-or-no basis. If they can all say yes to one or more of the packages, then the closure phase can begin. Any of the agreeable packages can become the basis for further refinement and definition of details, and, ultimately, agreement.

Of course, if all parties have been involved in designing the various deal packages, they would all presumably be in a position to agree to all of them. The yes-no vote might be a refinement, but presumably all of the deal packages could be in the ballpark of feasible solutions. If, on the other hand, one party had the mission of designing a series of deal packages and presenting them to the other for consideration, or if a third-party consultant or facilitator played that role, one or more of the negotiators might find some of them unacceptable. If none of the deal packages survive the yes-no appraisal, it is presumably possible to invent others, paying closer attention to the value elements that offered the most and least appeal to them.

Let's see how that works in practice. We were negotiating an agreement with a subject-matter expert to have him write a book that we would publish and market through our business catalog. Having explored the joint and separate interests involved, we had arrived at the point of having three quite different deal packages that we had prepared for his consideration. Because we had designed them, we already knew they represented a balance of interests from our point of view. We were not sure, of course, whether he would feel the same way.

We asked, "Would you please review these three variations, each of which emphasizes a different type of focus, and tell us if any or all of them appeal to you?" In this particular case, he felt that all three variations were fair, balanced, and could suit his needs. His response was, "All three of them offer more than I anticipated, so I can be happy with any one of them. Why don't you choose the one that suits you best?"

We chose one that we preferred and the deal was done. The fact that we had taken the trouble to share and explore interests at the outset and that we had worked to maintain a state of empathy throughout the discussions contributed to the generous spirit on both sides. The negotiation never moved out of the comfort zone. There were no offers and counteroffers, no posturing, no name calling, no demands or concessions, and no impasses.

Obviously, not all negotiations can proceed so quickly or cordially, but it's worth thinking about the benefits that an open, cooperative, empathic context can produce.

Well, so much for the easy stuff. Let's consider for a moment the kinds of approaches to evaluating deal packages that are necessary for large and complex negotiations. Suppose the option tree has dozens of variations, involving value factors like marketing rights and royalties, exchanges of stock for cash, deferred payments of funds, rights to use widely respected brand names, protection from competition for specified periods, financial risks due to political contingencies in a foreign country, and nonrefundable advances? Can the AVN approach make sense out of such a complex situation?

Not only can it make sense out of the situation, but this is also where it shines the most. The more complex and diversified the negotiation, the more you need a careful analysis of the value factors involved. Let's consider some examples.

Suppose you are an author negotiating a book contract with a publisher. One of the options for you under the category of money, in the subcategory of royalties, is the size of the advance. Here is an interesting trade-off. Advances paid by the publisher to the author are deducted from the royalties his or her book eventually earns. The author gets some money up front and starts collecting the remainder when the book's sales pass the point where it "earns out" the advance. In most publishing fields, these royalty advances are nonrefundable. This means that if the book never sells enough copies to earn out, the author nevertheless keeps the advance.

You might think it would always be in your best interest to have a high advance, because this would practically force the publisher to market the book well enough to recover the advance plus a profit. Just so. Yet, the publisher tends to favor a small advance because of the exact same logic. How do you reconcile both interests, and how do you figure out what the advance is really worth?

Imagine that one of the deal packages you and the publisher are considering has a relatively high advance payment and a relatively low royalty percentage, that is, the percentage of the book's earnings to be paid to you. Imagine also that another deal package offers you a higher royalty percentage along with a lower advance payment. How do you compare the value to you of the two different deal packages? You simply have to first make some estimate of the numbers of copies the book might sell over its lifetime. Using that figure, you calculate your total revenue from the advance and the royalty percentage for each of the two deal packages and see which one pays you more.

Now, an element of strategy comes into play. Suppose the book actually sells very few copies. Calculating the revenue from a low advance but a high royalty percentage, you might discover that the bigger advance is best for you. On the other hand, suppose the book jumps off the shelf and sells like chocolate chip cookies. The higher royalty percentage would then be better, even if the advance payment is lower. You'll eventually collect more than the advance because of the volume of sales.

This simple example contains virtually all of the ingredients for estimating the value to either party inherent in any deal package. Some might involve more complex calculations, but the logic is basically the same.

Is the other party interested in licensing your widget to sell in Germany? Look at some plausible estimates of the possible sales volumes in Germany, and you'll have a fairly rational basis for estimating the value of those rights. Are they interested in all of Europe, or the entire EC market? Again, estimate the possible sales volumes to get some sort of fix on the value of the rights. The Germany option could be worth so much, and the EC option could be worth something else. Now you have a basis, however approximate, for comparing the value of the two options for you.

You or the other party will also need to estimate the value of the rights to them. Given the same estimates of sales volumes, what will be their likely marketing costs, manufacturing costs, and costs of fees paid to you? The remainder is what the rights are worth to them.

One straightforward way to estimate the monetary value of some option to one of the parties is in terms of avoided cost. For example, you may be offering a one-of-a-kind specialized software system for possible trade in one of the deal packages. What's it worth to them? The avoided-cost rationale says it's worth whatever it would otherwise cost them to create something that offers the same benefits.

Why is an established small business likely to be worth more, if it's profitable, than the simple costs of buying the exact same equipment and renting similar premises? Because of the embedded knowledge and decisions that make it successful. Intuition alone can tell you that the mistakes you'll make and the logistical setbacks you'll have in starting a business from scratch will cost you something. That something has already been paid for in the successful business. It also has an established customer base, which the start-up business will somehow have to match. An estimate of the income and expenses for the start-up option, compared to the actuals of the established business, will give you an idea of the difference in value between the two options.

Keep in mind that one particular element of value might represent a money value to one party and a cost to another. Licensing your widget for marketing in Germany will bring you money, but it will cost the other party money. It will be necessary to find an element of value for them that makes the expenditure worthwhile. Note that it doesn't necessarily have to come from your pocket. For example, their profit, which is their balancing payoff, comes from the customers to whom they sell the widgets.

For this reason, many negotiations involve elements of value that cost one party little or nothing, and yet may represent enormous value to the other party. If you're not equipped to market your widget overseas, then anybody who can show you revenue from their efforts to do so is handing you found money. It makes sense to take careful inventory of the elements of value in any situation to see whether you have such no-cost options that can enrich the deal and get you a great deal of balancing value in return. Conversely, think about things the other party might be able to supply at no or low cost that might have enormous value to you and for which you would be willing to add balancing value.

The ideal situation, of course, is one in which all parties can contribute added value for one another at little or no cost to themselves. You might be surprised to learn how often this can be the case.

Certainly, there will be various options in various value categories that are subjective and which seem to defy any kind of normative analysis. Remember to think twice before you declare something imponderable in terms of its value. How about the right to use a highly respected brand identity in connection with a marketing effort? Again, it may be possible to analyze the two possible cases, one with the marque and one without it. Get some expert opinions on the difference in customer acceptance and the likely difference in sales levels. Convert this into an appropriate money figure and at least you have something more concrete to consider.

Not all elements of value are best evaluated in terms of money. Often it's enough to assess something in terms of its relationship to something else of recognized value. You might consider your colleague's Erté lithograph to have just about the same personal and aesthetic value as your Dali lithograph. If the two of you agree, then that's the measure of value that makes sense.

You can get a fix on a highly subjective element of value by thinking about what you would be willing to trade for it. If you had a choice between having custody of a famous old-master work of art for permanent display in your corporate boardroom and the prestige of having a famous personality sitting on your board of directors, which would you take? Maybe you would like to have both, but the point here is to get some sense of how you evaluate various elements of value.

The outcome of the evaluation stage of the AVN process is a reasoned appraisal of the value offered by each of the various deal packages to the respective parties in the negotiation. It is not your responsibility to evaluate the deal packages for the other parties, but at the very least you need to understand what they have to offer to you. It may also be worthwhile to help the others make their own evaluations if they haven't done so, to be sure they are clear about the choices they must make.

The tools and techniques of the evaluation phase can range all the way from a paper placemat from the coffee shop to computer spreadsheets and detailed financial analyses. In the end, if the negotiation is at least moderately large and complex, you will probably want to have a written appraisal or at least a grid chart of some sort that compares the various deal packages to one another in terms of their total value to you.

In many cases, the dividing line between evaluating the deal packages and actually choosing one may be invisible. A quick discussion might point the way to one deal package that appeals strongly to all concerned, or a brief pencil-and-paper analysis may satisfy everyone that a particular deal serves their interests best. In other cases involving large and complex negotiations, this round of the meet-and-confer cycle may end with a formal document describing the various deal packages, and the parties involved may choose to retire to their respective home bases and study them in detail. Then they can repeat the meet-and-confer cycle to begin converging on a feasible deal that they can refine into a final agreement.

PATIENCE: IF THEY SAY NO, COME UP WITH MORE DEALS

What do you do when you present four or five well-balanced deal packages, which you believe represent value for all parties to the negotiation, and someone says no to all of them? Suppose, for example, you're trying to work out an agreement to set up juice-bar kiosks in a chain of fitness centers. You've had several meet-and-confer cycles with them, identified the interests, itemized the various elements of value and the options for combining them, and you've constructed your deal packages. They say no. No to Deal A, no to Deal B, no to Deal C, no to Deal D.

What do you do? You come up with some more deal packages and try again. This is the elegantly simple part of added value negotiating. No does not mean never; it just means not now. It means not for this particular set of options. By offering options, you can keep the other person in his or her comfort zone. You're not offering one take-it-or-leave-it proposal that they will feel obliged to counterattack. You're offering a range of alternatives, and they're free to take one or more of them or to leave all of them. There are plenty more where those came from.

Actually, it doesn't make sense to just turn around and come up with more options and try again. The first step should be to find out why the deal packages you offered failed to appeal to them. The answer to this question can be very revealing and very important to the progress of the deal and the relationship.

Maybe one or more of the deal packages comes close to meeting their interests. Maybe a few small adjustments could make it attractive to them without losing its appeal for you. Maybe there are elements of one deal package that, if combined with elements of another, could appeal to everyone involved.

Maybe you just misperceived the connections between the elements of value in the option tree and the interests of the parties. What appealed to you while thinking on their behalf may not appeal to them.

Perhaps you could have been mistaken about the relative value of some of the options you included in the deal packages. You could have overestimated the worth of some options and underestimated the worth of others.

In any case, the logical approach would be to confer with them again about interests and options, get yourself reoriented, and then design some additional deal packages. After all, even the simplest negotiation can have literally thousands of possible combinations of the elements in the option tree.

On the other hand, the lack of acceptance of any of the proposed deal packages could signal a deeper and more significant problem for the negotiation, especially if it has been a rather difficult process so far. It could be that one party has not been honest about his or her real interests. A reluctance to respond to the various value propositions could signal a hidden interest that they have not shared. In such a case, you had better look at the very basis of the negotiation and find out whether the parties are indeed dealing in good faith.

Another useful approach when you're having trouble getting consensus on the arrangement of value in the deal packages is to ask the reluctant party to design one or more deal packages for your consideration. This can be a way of gaining insight into their views of the negotiation and their preferences for packaging value.

There is one possible reaction that you should not tolerate on the part of the other side, because it completely contradicts the spirit and philosophy of AVN. That is the practice of cherry picking—choosing the most favorable options from several different deals and trying to force them into one overbalanced deal that favors only their interests. Attempts to cherry-pick the option tree usually signal a win-lose attitude about negotiating, which you may already have detected at earlier stages of the process.

The win-lose negotiator says, "I don't like any of those deals. However, if you'll include option C from this deal and option E from this deal and put them into this other deal, I'll take it.'' Of course they would. Who wouldn't? But what added value negotiating is all about is the search for mutual and balanced value.

There is a very simple method for dealing with the cherry picker. It's a one-word response: ''No.'' This is another key strength of the added value negotiating method. You can always say no, just as the other party can say no. Saying no doesn't mean the negotiation is over. It just means it has to take another cycle of creating options for value. Once you can say no comfortably, assertively, and without antagonism, you are fully in control of your role in the process and you can easily repeat the previous step of designing more deal packages.

Of course, everything said so far assumes the negotiation is proceeding reasonably successfully along a track toward some consensus. If it isn't, if empathy problems have set in, or if it is becoming clear the other party is not accepting an added value philosophy in the situation, you have to go to the fundamental level of the relationship itself. You must either restore the relationship to a condition of empathy, reorient one or all parties toward an added value frame of reference, or else decide whether to continue with the negotiation.

In most cases, however, you will probably find that the process of designing alternative deal packages and going over them with the others leads you to a degree of consensus on which you can build a final agreement. After that comes the phase of perfecting the deal, working out the fine points, and getting to the ultimate handshake.

KEY INGREDIENT #5: TRUST THE PROCESS

With diligence and perhaps a bit of luck, you'll probably find that most of the negotiations you enter into will proceed fairly positively using these methods. We all must recognize, however, that a certain small percentage of individuals are selfish and self-centered to the extent that they simply refuse to negotiate from value. Working with them, the added value negotiating method will be no worse than the standard win-lose method, although it may not be much better. It may only offer you the peace of mind of knowing that you did your best to negotiate fairly and assertively. You may have to decide to walk away from the engagement, or, under some circumstances, you may decide to tough it out and settle for some sort of reasonably balanced deal, even if it isn't really an added value one.

You may find certain other people difficult to deal with as well, but not necessarily impossible. These are, perhaps, the more interesting cases. These are the ones who will challenge your added value negotiating skills, your understanding of the method, and your commitment to the philosophy of it. These are the folks who sort of understand it, and yet who have strong regressive tendencies to retreat to the familiar push-and-shove methods and game-playing tactics.

There is one important piece of advice for dealing with these middle-ground negotiators: Trust the process. The more experience you have with AVN, the easier and more instinctive you will find that it becomes. In the early stages of learning the AVN process, you may find that your own reflexes tend to pull you back toward the old ways. Be conscious of these impulses and think carefully about the situation at hand.

Once you have made a firm personal commitment to the idea of added value as an important precept in human life and in business, you will probably find that you're no longer satisfied with yourself when you resort to the pushing contest with other people. You will begin to hold yourself to a higher standard, even in the face of very difficult behavior on their part. Then you may go through a phase of self-doubt, wondering whether the commitment to added value isn't just a bit too idealistic. If it is really possible, why can't you do it perfectly every time? You just can't.

Added value negotiating is a philosophy, a personal commitment, and a practical method, but it isn't a cure-all. It isn't a magic wand or a sure-fire trick for getting other people to be reasonable. It can't change people's personalities, although it can sometimes bring out the best in them. It can't stop people from being unreasonable or even acting counter to their own overall interests, although it can sometimes entice them into recognizing that the pie can be made bigger just as easily as it can be cut smaller.

We have experienced this personal dilemma a number of times in dealing with difficult people, and we have discovered a certain peace of mind that comes from trusting the process. After all, you always have two fall-back options: (1) the power of your veto and (2) the right not to negotiate at all. There aren't too many deals that you really must have.

When things get complicated, when the process bogs down, when people behave unreasonably, and when progress seems slow, it's time to go right back to your first principles. In the middle of a very trying negotiation, it's a good idea to review the five steps in the added value negotiating process, right from the beginning. To do so, ask yourself:

- Have I really identified the various interests of the parties involved, and do I really understand how those interests are influencing the way they behave?
- Do I understand my own interests, and am I being honest about what I need to meet those interests?
- Am I doing everything I can to build and maintain a condition of empathy with them, within the boundaries of negotiating fairly and assertively?
- Have I succeeded in identifying the important elements of value available to the parties involved, and do I understand the various options for the exchange of value?
- Have I used good judgment in designing deal packages and offering them for consideration?
- Have I shown the kind of fairness, openness, and flexibility I would like them to show?

There may be a few situations in which you'll feel there is little point in proceeding, but, if there is still hope, we believe the process will never let you down if you apply it honestly, openly, fairly, and assertively.

DEALING WITH DIRTY TRICKS, NASTY GIMMICKS, AND BATTLEFIELD TACTICS

Just to make sure we've dealt realistically with the most difficult forms of negotiating behavior you're likely to meet, it's worthwhile to take inventory of the dirty tricks some people learn in their negotiating seminars and work out some approaches that may help in dealing with them.

If you have any experience with negotiating at all, through books, audio or video tapes, training seminars, or personal knowledge, you've probably come across some of the tricks, tactics, and gambits listed below. Some of them are outright deceptions, bent on separating you from your money, others fall into the oops-I-didn't-mean-to-let-you-catch-me-at-that category, and some of them are just plain mean in spirit and deed.

Most of the other win-lose negotiating books, tapes, and seminars go into some detail describing these tricks, offering the best times for you to use them. As we feel that these so-called power tricks and traps violate the true spirit of added value negotiating, we advise against their use.

As you review this list of 20 entries, try to recall from your past negotiating experiences whether you've encountered any of them. Some of these may have been forced on you during your last major purchase—a car, a house, furniture, etc. Others may have appeared during a crucial business or contractual negotiation, and others may have popped up during personal negotiations or during conflict resolution sessions.

Most of these tactics have not changed in decades. Probably the old maxim "If something works, stick with it" is the reason many of these old negotiating dinosaurs have hung on. They seem to be a popular part of the curriculum for many negotiating training seminars, so much so that many people think that they are what negotiating is really all about.

See if you recognize any of these tricks:

The afterbite. Requesting or demanding something extra after you've already signed the deal. Sometimes the party who drafts the written agreement will tuck in all sorts of standard provisions that were never part of the negotiation.

The baseball bat. Putting some form of pressure on you, outside the scope of the negotiation, such as legal attacks, competitive actions, etc., that limit the options available within the negotiation.

Blanketing. Loading up the negotiation session with tons of paper, spreadsheets, analyses, and dozens of team members so you feel physically intimidated by the sheer numbers.

Bracketing. This is usually a price-oriented technique designed to pin you down to a figure. Car salespeople like to ask, "How much do you want to pay a month?" rather than deal over the actual price of the car.

Deadlines. Here the other party uses time to put pressure on you. Sellers will try to force you to act before a certain date and buyers will say that they plan to talk to a competitor, or that the money won't be available after a certain date.

Delaying action. Stalling or dragging out the negotiations to cause problems in one or more of your interest areas, or to buy time to negotiate with your competitors.

False information. Outright lying; presenting false data or making false claims to get you to change your position.

False withdrawal. The other side appears to withdraw from the negotiations, only to continue working on the deal behind your back. Often used to express interest in another deal completely, while waiting for an appropriate moment to re-enter the negotiations at a more tactical moment.

The feint. Diverting attention from the real issues in order to confuse things. Focusing energy on a particular topic to make you think it's important and divert your attention from the one they consider crucial.

Fine print. Inserting seemingly innocuous provisions into a written agreement that weren't part of the original deal, but which add value for the other party.

Funny money. Hidden costs or charges never mentioned until after that jack up the final cost of the deal including taxes, shipping charges, dock fees, handling charges, copying fees, document fees, and unseen commissions.

Good guy/bad guy. A classic technique, pitting the seemingly hostile negotiator against you while his or her nicer partner tries to intervene. You may be so put off by the bad guy that you'll agree to the offer made by the good guy.

Hi-ball/lo-ball. Starting with an unreasonably high or low price figure and expecting you to beat them back to a more reasonable position.

Intimidation. Physical tactics, situations, or environments intended to make you feel insignificant, subordinate, or less powerful than the other party. Examples include employing physically large, loud, aggressive, or bullying negotiators; smoke-filled meeting rooms; conducting negotiations in a very imposing, opulent setting; male condescension toward females; and calling meetings at times and places that create travel stress and jet lag for you.

Limited authority. The "I can't decide (or close the deal) without talking to my boss/partner/associate/spouse" approach. This places the blame for aggressive tactics on some invisible third party and allows the spokesperson to pretend to be responding to direction from elsewhere.

Nibbling. The "if you can't get dinner, get a sandwich" technique. The other side will ask you for some small item or additional piece to the deal, hoping you'll give in because you don't want to blow the whole deal over a trivial item.

Salami. Negotiating piece by piece, item by item, rather than from the big picture. The "one slice at a time" strategy, often used to price separate parts of the same deal.

Silence. Here the other party will use silence in two ways: as either a sign of your implied consent (if you don't object it must be okay), or as a means of drawing you out to give up more concessions.

Surprise. A sudden position shift from the other side that throws you for a loop. Usually a dramatic or drastic change in the price or in their approach that catches you off guard. Often used against you when you introduce a new piece of information to the negotiation.

Take it or leave it. The other party presents certain demands and indicates that that is the only deal he or she is prepared to make.

In most cases, the best ways to respond to these tricks, traps, and tactics is to recognize them for what they are and then gracefully sidestep them. A response that is innocent, fair, and assertive can often derail the attack completely. There are a few reliable responses you might find helpful and not antagonistic:

"Calling" the behavior. You explicitly refer to what the other party has done, and make it an element of the negotiation. When the other party puts in an afterbite while writing up the agreement, you can just say, "Oh! I noticed you included some elements that we hadn't discussed during the negotiation. I didn't realize they were important to you. We'd be happy to reopen the discussion and see how we can accommodate you in exchange for some added value on your part."

Asking for objective support. Insist that any element of value requested or demanded be backed up by a good logical reason for its inclusion. This applies especially to money figures that are not based on any particular logic. If they use the take-it-or-leave-it ploy by saying, "I want $100,000 cash up front," you can say, "A hundred thousand dollars, eh? That's an interesting figure. How did you arrive at that figure as the monetary value of the arrangement?" If they say, "It's none of your business," you can say, "I understand why you might be reluctant to tell me, but I have to tell you that it's unacceptable to me unless I can see some objective support for it."

Asking for a quid pro quo. Insist politely that any additional request or demand be balanced by some form of value offered to you. If they use the nibble technique after you've reached agreement and say, "And just one more thing—we'll expect you to pay for the shipping on returned merchandise," you can say, "I can see why that would be valuable to you. If you'd like to add that into the agreement, what do you propose to add to make that worthwhile for us?"

Sticking to the big picture. A key strength of added value negotiating is that it allows trade-offs by using a wide-angle lens to include all elements of the deal in the discussion. If they try to use the salami approach and say, "Let's work out the discount arrangement first; then we can move on to the less important issues," you can say, "I'm sorry, but we consider all of the issues as part of the same big picture.

We're willing to trade one option for another, but we're not willing to negotiate on a piecemeal basis."

Time out. Calling for a pause in the discussions so you can collect your thoughts and reconsider all parts of the situation. If they throw in a surprise element by saying, "Incidentally, we're also negotiating with your competitors on this issue; we'll expect your fees to be lower than theirs," you can say, "Oh! That puts a new light on the matter. I thought we were negotiating in good faith, but it appears you're basically just priceshopping at this point. Maybe we'd better postpone the rest of the discussion and get together again when you've completed your talks with Company X."

The Japanese word *judo* translates roughly into "the gentle way" in English. The technique of judo involves deftly redirecting the energy of the attacker and either neutralizing it or turning it back against the attacker. That's what these simple reaction patterns are—added value judo.

It's surprising how often these five simple tactics can neutralize the negative energy of the negotiator who believes in the win-lose or disguised win-lose approach. Without aggression, without hostility, and without manipulation, you simply redirect the energy toward the objective of a balanced agreement. Innocence and transparency, coupled with an attitude that is both fair and assertive, can have powerful effects. They are not weapons, and yet they can accomplish what weapons often cannot.

WHEN AND HOW TO WALK AWAY

Even at this point, there must certainly be some readers who are thinking, "No matter how positively you paint the picture of added value negotiating, we all know there are some people who are so toxic, so demanding and domineering, and so unwilling to cooperate that there is really no point in trying to negotiate with them. Does added value negotiating allow for the circumstance when you have to vote with your feet?"

It certainly does. You'll know when the time comes. The only question is one of style. Do you stomp out of the meeting, send a nasty letter, and call a press interview to tell the world what dirty birds they are or do you simply call a halt to the process and send the other party on his or her way with the best wishes you can muster?

The choice is up to you, and it will reflect your own personal world-view about these things. In the long run, it may not matter, but in the short run you might want to think about the best way to do it.

Probably our favorite way is a simple, unequivocal statement: "Well, it looks like we won't be able to do business." Said without rancor, offered in the best spirit of a search for joint value, and presented with a simple air of straightforward communication of a fact, it tells the tale. In our view, there is little point in haranguing the other party about their unwillingness to cooperate, or their dishonesty, or their lack of character, or any of a dozen other possible accusations. It's time to stop wasting your time and let them stop wasting theirs.

We don't believe it's usually a good idea to bluff about ending a negotiation. Some people advocate this, and we can understand their view. From our point of view, however, bluffing is an admission to yourself that you've lost control of your side of the situation, and you've resorted to the same kinds of interpersonal tactics the other side uses.

On occasion, it may be worthwhile to test the possibilities for continuing. You might want to say, "Look, I've been thinking about this whole situation. We don't seem to be getting anywhere and we're all getting stressed. Do you think we ought to agree to disagree, and just call it a day?"

Bear in mind also that some negotiations are difficult and ill fated not because anyone is acting inhumanely, but because an agreement is just not in the cards. The interests may not be sufficiently overlapped to make a reasonable deal possible. This doesn't mean you can't do business some time in the future on some other matter. In that case, it may be important to wind up the discussions on a cordial note if possible, thereby leaving open the opportunity to get together on some other occasion.

If you're the kind of person who values positive feelings between human beings for their own sake and strives to maintain them whenever possible, agreeing to disagree can be almost as valuable and affirming a process as agreeing to agree.

Chapter Eight

Getting to the Handshake:
Perfecting the Deal

"I don't condone it, certainly, but there's nothing in our code of ethics that specifically forbids it."

The fifth step in the added value negotiating process is perfecting the deal. Assuming you've had good success—or good luck in some cases—with the first four steps, you now have a deal that is fairly attractive to all parties concerned. It offers value to all in reasonably balanced measure, and the parties are still all in one piece both physically and psychically.

There is still some important work that needs to be done. Now it's time
to fine-tune the deal and set up things to ensure its success.

ADDING CREATIVE REFINEMENTS

A good deal is never really complete. At least that's the general attitude
of added value negotiating. If you've been able to maintain a high level
of empathy with the other party and both sides feel they gained in value
as the negotiation moved along, both are likely to be in a mood to continue adding value for each other. Extra touches, creative refinements and
cooperative gestures are always possible, even if only in small ways.

Note that these added value refinements are not the same as concessions, as generally defined. You are not conceding anything; you are adding something if possible, and there is a big difference. This particular
precept of added value negotiating directly contradicts the traditional
win-lose approach, which dictates that you should never yield anything
without getting something of equal or greater value in return.

The final touches and refinements serve the purpose of building, reinforcing, and maintaining empathy. They are not a part of the process of
designing deals; you've already done that. If you don't have a good deal
at this point, refinements will not be enough to salvage it. These are typically elements of small but symbolic value.

If the negotiation has not been as comfortable as you would have
liked, you might find that neither party is in a particularly generous
mood. In that case, you may not feel inclined to think creatively about
adding anything extra. On the other hand, you might feel that a small
gesture of some kind might soften bruised feelings and help to restore
empathy to some extent.

Just be sure you know why you're doing what you're doing. Making
concessions in order to get the other party in a better mood is usually not
a good idea. A better idea is to deal directly with the reasons for the bad
mood. Do they have doubts about the value they're receiving? Do they
have reason to mistrust you or feel you're not sharing important information? Do they feel they've been treated unkindly or disrespectfully
when communicating with you? It may be helpful to back up one or two
steps in the process and get things reoriented so both parties can feel
right about what's happening.

Added value negotiating works from the heart and the head at the
same time. When you negotiate both fairly and assertively, maintain a

high level of empathy, and respond generously, you are being true to your highest personal values as well as getting a good deal while you're at it.

DEALING WITH POST-NEGOTIATION GIMMICKS

Even under the best of negotiating circumstances, people can be tempted to get tricky, and in the most difficult situations you can expect it. By holding fast to the basic ethical stance of added value negotiating, you can anticipate some of the last-minute tricks and gimmicks, and you can deal with them fairly and assertively. Some of these gimmicks come from people who negotiate competitively or combatively. Others come from simple innocence or inexperience, that is, from people who think they're supposed to grab every possible opportunity to get a little more for their side. You can take these last-minute ploys in stride rather than overreacting.

The best way to deal with postnegotiation trickery is to prevent it from arising. This is not always a completely realistic expectation, but it is usually a worthwhile objective. One thing you can do to steer people away from these behaviors is to make yourself predictable to them all along the road of the negotiating process.

If you model openness and transparency, if you allow the process to carry the negotiation, if you concentrate on value and refuse to personalize or emotionalize the process, and if you deal with each question of value fairly and assertively, they soon learn how you operate. They are less likely to use tricks such as the afterbite and the fine print if they know you scrutinize all elements of value and expect to resolve all issues in a balanced way.

Nevertheless, it does help to recognize and deal with the most common postnegotiation gimmicks. Let's take a look at each of them, along with a reasonable countermeasure. To keep the discussion simple, let's classify them into four basic categories, in order of severity:

1. The afterbite. One party asks for one or more extra elements of value after the first handshake. *Example*: "By the way, we'll need a complete set of samples of all products in your line, along with data sheets for sales purposes." *Countermeasure*: Reopen the negotiating process. Go back to the process of designing deals and offer to include this element of added value in exchange for something they can add. You might say, "I can see why that would be valuable to you, but we haven't discussed it so far, and it would represent a significant cost to us. How do you see us being compensated for those costs?" You'll find that this exact same countermeasure, in one form or another, can deal effectively with most postnegotiation gimmicks.

2. The fine print. One party volunteers to write up the agreement and takes the opportunity to tuck in various elements of value not discussed. This is a variation of the afterbite, except that it's done surreptitiously. *Example*: the fine print in an author's book contract may say "Publisher will have the right of first option to publish Author's next work, and will have no obligation to exercise said right until 12 months after publication of the present work, or 12 months after presentation of Author's proposal, whichever is later." This gives "Publisher" as much as two years to make a decision, during which time "Author" is prevented from offering a new book to any other publisher. *Countermeasure*: Reopen the negotiation.

Actually, the example given is a variation we call the sacrificial lamb ploy. This amounts to putting in a provision with no real intention of fighting for it just to create the appearance of a concession when the other party rejects it. This is one of the significant advantages of added value negotiating over positional negotiating. You don't deal in demands and concessions, so every element of value must have a justification in a trade-off for some other element of value.

When the Author goes back to the Publisher offering to negotiate for the sacrificial lamb provision, both parties know the compensating value would have to be sky high. Publisher drops the clause because it wasn't really a legitimate item anyway.

3. Hidden assumptions. Provisions appear mysteriously in the written agreement, which the drafting party justifies as standard practices, or the "we naturally assumed . . . " ploy. Another cousin of the afterbite, this provision seems natural and normal enough, but will cost you something not contained in the deal package. *Example*: "We expect all of our real estate loan contracts to include mortgage insurance. It's a standard practice in this industry." *Countermeasure*: Reopen the negotiation. You might say, "It may indeed be standard practice, but you made no mention of it when we were discussing the various options for the deal. It's not acceptable to me under the present arrangement. How do you suggest we cover it?"

4. The take-back. A more extreme ploy, in which one person goes through the motions of negotiating and then resorts to a higher power for the decision not to ratify the deal the two of you made. *Example*: "Our board reviewed the arrangement we submitted, and they agree with everything except the term of the agreement. They want a five-year term instead of a three-year term. If that's OK with you, we can sign the contract." You need to analyze the options to see whether the change in the term affects the value you will receive from the deal. If it is not in your best interest, don't be done in by the "invisible negotiator." *Countermeasure*: Reopen the negotiation. Say, "I can understand why they would see a five-year term as more valuable for them than three years. On the other hand, the balance of value in the deal we worked out was based on three years. I'd be happy to discuss a five-year term if you can show me a way to make it worth my while."

Actually, the take-back ploy is often just a communication gimmick, so you will usually do best to treat it as merely a communication problem. The other player is hoping you'll give in rather than go through the red tape of communicating with The Board, The Commission, his or her Boss or Business Partner, or any other mysterious absent entity. Hoping to extract a last-minute concession by their own devices, they might even be lying about the hidden decision maker. The board may not know the first thing about the substance of the negotiation.

In these cases you simply offer to continue the process of designing deals and waiting for the other party to go through whatever rigmarole they choose. You can say no just as calmly and assertively as the Board said no. Let the other party know that if they have to go to some higher beings for approval, then the two of you are still in stage three of the process, that is, designing various deal packages. You're happy to continue this process until everybody is happy.

When the other party takes the matter to the mysterious higher beings, make sure they understand that you do not view this as an approval process. As far as you're concerned, it's merely a process of checking with the other parties to see how they feel about one possible deal package. If the Board hasn't approved the deal, then you haven't either. While you're all in the process of conferring with the higher beings, why not present them with multiple deal packages instead of just one hoped-for "final" deal, especially in view of the fact that your negotiating counterpart apparently can't do the handshake anyway?

Refusing to be intimidated by some distant higher authority and re-fusing to be placed in the role of a supplicant to their authority system can often move your negotiating counterpart to a more practical, results-oriented mode of operation. When your counterpart knows you aren't intimidated by the authority front, you may find that he or she becomes remarkably good at persuading the board that the deal package you've worked out together is the best one.

For each of the types of postnegotiation ploys just discussed, you can see that the same countermeasure applies: reopen the negotiation and seek balancing value in exchange for what they've asked. Actually, it isn't even a countermeasure; it's just the added value negotiating method at work: openness, transparency, empathy, proceeding on interests, fo-cusing on value, concentrating on a balance of value, being patient and designing deal packages until one or more of them fits the interests of the parties involved.

ASSURING ACCEPTANCE: AVOIDING NEGOTIATOR'S REMORSE

You may occasionally find that the person with whom you're dealing gets an attack of negotiator's remorse, similar to buyer's remorse on the part of someone who has just paid a lot of money for a major item of purchase. There are last-minute doubts. Am I doing the right thing? Did I get a good deal? Should I have asked for more? Am I being tricked?

You might feel these doubts yourself sometimes, although the AVN method should help you keep a clear focus on your interests all along the way. The other party on the other hand might not always be so mentally clear and confident. Friends or associates may offer him or her their advice. They may suspect that, because the negotiation has pro-ceeded amicably, their friend or associate must be getting taken for a ride; otherwise there would be more shouting, pushing, and shoving go-ing on. They may assume that any potential deal package you might offer must have some cushion in it to allow you to make concessions when the real negotiating starts. They may urge your counterpart to demand more from you.

Patience, not surprisingly, is an important virtue in this final stage of the process. Even though we are thinking of the fifth stage as one of refining and perfecting the selected deal, you must always be ready, willing, and able to back up one or more steps so you can rethink it and consider others.

Again, the best way to deal with negotiator's remorse is to prevent it from afflicting you or your counterpart. First, think of the most likely reasons for the affliction:

- Lack of negotiating experience and contamination of one's views of the process by the combative values of the surrounding culture.
- Self-doubt, low self-confidence, and a weak self-image; the person may just feel insecure and personally powerless and may feel uncomfortably dependent on you to be fair.
- Insufficient homework or insufficient understanding of their own interests; the other person may not have a clear picture of his or her own personal objectives and may not have thought through the needs and benefits associated with the possible deal.
- Insuffient use of the AVN process; either or both of you neglects to work through all of the steps in the process, with the result that the later steps lack the basic clarity needed to bring matters to consensus.
- Existence of one or more uncertainty factors in the other person's situation that make it difficult to assess the potential value of some of the deal packages. One deal might be better if A happens, while another might be better if B happens; they choose A but worry that B might really happen.

With these most common causes of negotiator's remorse in mind, we can see that the best antidote to the affliction is clarity. The better you have defined the interests involved, the better you have identified and classified the elements of value open to exchange. Similarly, the better you have evaluated the various deal packages in terms of how well they meet the interests, the less doubt there is likely to be in the minds of the negotiators.

The best way to achieve and maintain this kind of clarity is, of course, to work with the process. By following through on each of the first three or four steps, you can get to the fifth step with enough understanding, data, and information to allow all of the players involved to make informed choices. Be willing to back up to any earlier stage in the process to restore clarity and understanding. Make it clear that the process can easily move in either direction, and that you do not seek a deal for the sake of a deal; you seek an exchange of value that meets the interests of all of the parties to the negotiation.

Another useful technique for enhancing clarity is to review the interests and options from time to time as you proceed through the process. For example, when you have completed the second step of defining value and classifying the options on the option tree, meet and confer with the other party to review both interests and options. Discuss them in depth and make sure all parties perceive them accurately.

When you move to the third step, designing various deal packages, keep referring to the interests and options so you will stay focused on possibilities that have the best chance of appealing to all parties. Put together several deal packages that are quite different and that offer balanced value in various interesting ways. Before you ask the other party to evaluate the deals, meet and confer to discuss each of them in depth. Make sure everyone involved understands what each deal package would entail and that they can clearly evaluate each one against their stated interests.

Finally, make sure your communicating style during the process enables the other party to be comfortable in making choices without a sense of pressure or undue persuasion. You don't have to sell them on any particular deal. You only have to come up with one or more deals on which you both can agree.

DEAL INSURANCE: MAKING SURE THE DEAL DOESN'T COME UNSTUCK

Another important part of the fifth stage of added value negotiating is safeguarding the deal—making sure it doesn't come unstuck. Having a good deal package as a basis for positive discussions between the parties is not enough to ensure a successful outcome. You have to manage the negotiating situation all along the way to make sure the deal actually becomes a reality.

Just as in dealing with negotiator's remorse, dealing with end-of-the-road pitfalls deserves a good measure of prevention. You need to think about the kinds of malfunctions that can occur, how to prevent them, and how to handle them if they arise anyway. Early in the process and on a fairly frequent basis along the way, you need to double-check the basic elements that can spell danger or success. Ask yourself the following questions:

- Am I fully in control of my side of the negotiation? Am I likely to be ambushed or thwarted by principals to whom I must answer? Do I have their full backing and support?

- Is my negotiating counterpart fully empowered to make the deal or is he or she just a point of contact for a complex decision-making process?

- Is a deal really a deal or might there be some final review by mysterious higher beings on the other side?

- Are all of the stakeholders in this affair actually at the table? Are all of them involved in the discussions? Might there be external parties whose actions or reactions could thwart the intent of the negotiation?

- Is the deal we're working on actually do-able? Is it legal? Is it politically possible? Is it logistically, economically, and technically feasible?

- Do we have a means of communication among the parties that supports open discussion of options and arrival at a consensus? Are there missing links, problem relationships, or breakdowns in understanding?

- Do we have a reasonable condition of empathy to support the search for mutual value? Are all parties in a reasonably cooperative state of mind?

- Are the parties to the negotiation willing to work from an added value perspective, or do some of them present difficult negotiating styles? Are they pushing, demanding, and manipulating instead of communicating and reasoning together? Are they withholding information rather than sharing it and using it to the best advantage?

By realistically assessing the state of the negotiating process at its various stages, you can decide whether it is heading for trouble. If you see danger signs, you can shift the focus from the content of the negotiation to the process itself. By ensuring a strong, cooperative process, you are usually ensuring that the deal it produces will actually become reality.

SHAKING HANDS: THE CEREMONY AND THE PAPERWORK

Think carefully about the effect of ritual, ceremony, and celebration in the negotiating process. Ceremonializing the deal can be a very important part. The amount of celebration that's appropriate will depend very much on the kind of deal at hand, that is, the scope and magnitude of the value involved, the number of players involved, the number of onlookers, and the significance of the deal to the parties involved and to other stakeholders.

We human beings need ritual, celebration, and ceremony in our lives. It is a form of symbolic communication that formalizes major changes in human experience. That's why we have weddings, birthdays, gradua-tions, retirement parties, and funerals. A ceremony is a public (or at least semipublic) signal that the people involved have experienced an impor-tant change in their lives, that they are accepting the change, and that they are acknowledging its impact in their experience.

The appropriate degree of ceremony can vary widely, from a simple handshake between two parties, to a special gathering of representatives of all parties, to a public handshake for the benefit of onlookers, all the way to a highly publicized handshake such as that involved in signing a treaty between two nations.

The documentation that goes with the deal can play a very important role as well. Even for small deals that don't justify formal treaties or elaborate contracts, putting things on paper in simple form can strengthen the commitment of all parties and prevent possible misunder-standing later. This can vary from a simple handwritten confirmation sent by one party to another, spelling out the key elements of the deal they have created, to a memo of understanding or letter of agreement and all the way to a formal contract or treaty.

It's a good idea to write down the basic elements of virtually every deal, even a very simple one. In the spirit of added value negotiating, putting the deal on paper has several benefits:

- Human beings have remarkably faulty memories; a few months after a verbal agreement, people can have amazingly disparate inter-pretations of what the agreement really meant. Hard copy prevents further dispute.
- The negotiators may have constructed the deal on behalf of other parties whom they represent; it is important for all stakeholders to review the written deal, to test their understanding of the deal, and to correct misunderstandings now rather than later.
- When you get to the stage of perfecting the deal, you may discover certain detailed considerations nobody thought of during the design phase. Writing up the deal brings these issues forward for careful

thought. You can usually settle the small ones easily, but if there are any sleeper issues that can substantially affect the structure of the deal, you may need to back up one or more steps and untangle them.

- Stress can change both people and circumstances; when the business venture fizzles and the partners are swimming in red ink, all of them may be tempted to reconstrue their memories of the deal in their own best interests. Many people tend to become cannibalistic in difficult economic times; when the pie is too small, they turn on one another. A good agreement accounts for the worst-case outcome even though it concentrates on the best case.

Returning to the topic of ceremony, we can see it as an integral part of the negotiating process not as an afterthought. The handshake, the written agreement, and even the early steps of implementing the deal are all part of the momentum of the AVN process. Too many books and seminars on negotiating stop when the boxing gloves come off, that is, when the agreement is basically complete. It is important to carry your thinking beyond the final structure of the deal to create a sense of commitment to action.

HOW TO AVOID LAWYERS

It is our firm personal conviction that every written agreement between human beings should be written in plain language. The "whereas" and "wherefore" language and the "party of the first part" and "party of the second part" constructions have no place in the communication of added value and human cooperation. They are the tools of obfuscators, and they serve no other purpose than to create job security for the obfuscators. This is nowhere more true than in the United States.

America is a country virtually obsessed with litigation. It is probably the most litigious society on earth. The United States has 26 times as many lawyers per 100,000 citizens as Japan has. Its courts are clogged with more civil cases than they can possibly process. It is one of the few Western countries that allows contingency pricing by attorneys, that is, the practice in which the attorney accepts the risk of success in exchange for a share of the damages collected. This has resulted in a legal system that concentrates almost solely on money as the measure of injury and recompense.

Lawyers operate more often as deal killers than deal builders. They are like pit bulls trained from birth to fight and to help others fight. It is a rare circumstance in which an attorney sees his or her mission as helping two people create the maximum value for each other. Indeed, the legal system they have forged may even make it impossible. In Western law, an attorney cannot represent both parties to a litigation, except under very narrowly defined circumstances. This means that he or she is automatically on the side of one or another of the parties to a deal. It becomes circumstantially almost impossible for that person to focus on value for both parties.

This is one reason why so many contracts and agreements among Americans have a distinctly adversarial tone and style. Look at a typical commercial real estate lease for, say, the rental of a shop in a mall. It will typically run to at least 30 pages, with provisions no ordinary human being other than a flaming paranoid would ever think of including. It even prescribes what will happen if the government or the national military force ever seizes the property for public use during a civil disturbance.

It goes on and on with provisions that paint the landlord as legally invincible and the tenant as having virtually no rights except the right to occupy the premises. It's difficult to read one of these things from the point of view of the customer, that is, the tenant, without feeling angry and defensive. It is an aggressive, disturbing document.

Bank loans work much the same way. The loan agreement starts by assuming that you're basically a crook and not to be trusted. Then it prescribes very narrowly what you get and don't get from the loan. Then it tells you what the bank gets to do to you if you don't live up to the terms. It's hard to feel like the bank is really your business partner, which is the advertising message the marketing people thought up to get your business.

Insurance policies are no fun to read, either. Many kinds of business agreements do nothing to reinforce a feeling of cooperation and added value in the mind of the person signing them. Indeed, most of them tend to make the the client feel defensive and apprehensive.

This is the legacy of legalism. We have a business environment in which people have long ago ceased making agreements on a handshake, where a person's word is no longer his or her bond. We have legal practitioners who are dedicated to minimizing value rather than adding value. We need to learn to communicate with one another in nonadversarial ways. We need to learn to build bridges of openness, clarity, and rational judgment that can help people achieve high-value consensus rather than minimum-value consensus. If we can stop negotiating as if we have platoons of lawyers looking over our shoulders and start communicating clearly and simply about interests and about value, we can all generate more value in our lives.

USING PLAIN-ENGLISH AGREEMENTS TO BUILD TRUST

When Charles A. Lindbergh, the famous American aviator, wanted an airplane for his solo transatlantic flight in 1927, he sent a telegram to aviation pioneer T. Claude Ryan in San Diego. According to aerospace historians the telegram said something like:

> "Can you build airplane that will fly nonstop from New York to Paris? If so, state price and delivery time."

Ryan fired back a telegram that said:

> "We can build airplane you require. Time is three months. Cost is six thousand dollars if you supply engine and instruments."

That was the beginning of one of the most famous incidents in aviation history. Many years later, when the U.S. federal government was considering a project for a supersonic transport plane, which it later abandoned, it asked the major aircraft companies for proposals. The government's invitation for bids ran to several hundred pages of dense prose, and the proposals submitted by both Lockheed and Boeing individually were stacks of reports taller than a fully grown person. This is progress?

One of the best-kept secrets in the business world is the plain-English agreement, or PEA. In international terms, it's the Plain-Language Agreement, or PLA. It's remarkable that, after so many centuries of business experience, Westerners still batter one another with elaborate, verbose, formal, legalistic, and boring documents that attempt to describe the exciting business ventures at hand. Overall, the best deals are simple deals, and by far the best agreements are simple agreements.

As you may have gathered from our mild-mannered discussion previously on the roles of lawyers in negotiating, we believe that the more elaborate the agreement and the more difficult it is for ordinary people to comprehend, the less valuable it is. We can no longer afford to operate on the assumption that if the lawyers understand it, it must be okay for the rest of us.

One of the Ten Commandments of Christian teaching is "Thou shalt not kill." Four words. Unambiguous. How do you think it would sound if a team of lawyers wrote it? Would it be more binding or less? In our experience, heavily loaded agreements with lots of intricate provisions tend to have *more* loopholes and areas of confusion, not fewer.

Legal opinions may vary on this point, but it is our view that PEAs can often be *more* legally binding than the longer and more elaborate agreements written in lawyerese. The reason is that ultimately any agreement really only means what a court says it means. If one party has to litigate to enforce the agreement, it will be up to the court to interpret what they said. The simpler the agreement, and the more clearly it explains the nature of the relationship they were trying to construct, the less able either party will be to evade its meaning in court. The spirit of the agreement will speak much louder than the letter of it.

With an agreement written in legalese, on the other hand, the court will have to play the role of semantic interpreter, and the settlement of the case might well hinge on the way it construes a particular phrase.

There are several good reasons for using PEAs in your negotiations:

- They tend to be shorter, more to the point, and easier for everyone to comprehend.
- Their provisions tend to be more memorable when stripped of unnecessary verbiage.
- Plain language tends to be much less threatening to most people than legal terminology. It helps to maintain empathy and reflect the underlying trust in the relationship.
- Simpler statements tend to be more comprehensive and less ambiguous, while more elaborate statements create the impression of leaving out whatever they have not explicitly mentioned.
- Writing a PEA forces you to be very clear about what you believe the parties have agreed to do.
- They are much easier to prepare and less taxing for the person preparing them.

You can use PEAs on at least three different levels of formality, even though the terminology can be quite informal in all cases:

1. Letter of understanding. This is a simple letter or memo sent by one person to another that outlines in plain language the elements of the agreement. Because it is a one-way communication, it isn't necessarily a binding contract, but it may be quite adequate for the needs of the parties involved.

2. Letter of agreement. This is a simple letter with room at the bottom for both parties to sign. It explains in simple language the nature of the arrangement in which they are involved and tells what each of them is entitled to and must do. A simple form of a letter of agreement (LOA) is a signed letter sent by one person to the other, with an invitation to the other person to sign both copies, keep one, and return the other. The separate copies become binding agreements.

3. Plain-English contract. This is a more extensive agreement, but still a simple one in style, structure, and terminology. It divides the provisions of the deal into logical topics or categories and simply states what the parties agreed to in each area. It might have an introductory paragraph or two to help the reader understand the nature of the deal. It might also spell out their individual interests so as to lend clarity to the explanation of the elements to follow.

In all cases, the PEA speaks on a person-to-person basis and uses commonplace terminology. A letter of understanding or a letter of agreement can use simple I-and-you language. The writer can speak in the first person and address the receiver in the second person. Using familiar, everyday language helps create a tone of cooperation and personal assurance. Keep the sentences short and to the point. Use contractions when convenient to lend a sense of informality, for example, "You'll provide the funds . . . " rather than "You will provide the funds. . . ."

A typical PEA letter of agreement might begin as follows:

Dear Joe,

This letter outlines my understanding of the agreement we've reached regarding the *XYZ* matter. If you agree with the provisions I've described below, please sign both copies, return one copy to me, and keep the other copy for your records.

We agree to the following points.

I will:

1. Point 1 (your part of the deal)
2. Point 2
3. Etc.

You will:
1. Point 1 (his or her part of the deal)
2. Point 2
3. Etc.

Both of us will:
1. Point 1 (joint provisions affecting both sides)
2. Point 2
3. Etc.

You may often find that a simple itemization of the elements of the deal, expressed in action terms, is quite enough to spell out everything. You don't have to write a detailed dissertation on every point. Just say what the other party will do, not do, receive, or be entitled to, and say the same for your side. Then cover any other provisions that affect both of you. Give it a cordial closing paragraph and you have a plain-English letter of agreement.

Keep in mind, too, that a good PEA will spell out the conditions for termination, if that should become appropriate. You should consider options for this as well as the other elements of value during the negotiation. Have you ever thought of termination as a value element under the option tree? Think of it as part of the category of rights. The right to get out of the deal has a value and therefore should be part of a trade-off. For example, terminating a five-year agreement after only one year might impose significantly more costs on Party A than on Party B, so the right to do so has more value to Party B. It makes sense to consider in advance how to allocate the risks and costs under such an option.

Think carefully before you agree to a provision that allows any of the parties to simply terminate the agreement on the assumption that the right to cancel it has equal value for all parties. You may want to link this right to the cumulative investment each party has made and to the prospective costs of termination. Consider also that, if the costs of getting out of an agreement are intolerably high, one party might simply fail to make good on his or her part of the deal and allow it to wither and fall into dispute. This could be more costly to the other parties than a simple termination.

Another important provision of the PEA is a simple, noncombative basis for resolving possible disputes between the parties about living up to it. Many informal business agreements leave this factor unmentioned, with the result that the parties may end up in costly legal battles. Some plain-English agreements specify that all parties agree not to litigate in case of disagreements, but rather to use some form of binding arbitration to settle disputes. This is often a peace-of-mind factor for both sides, as well as a way to limit the costs of settling arguments.

While you're capitalizing on the use of simple language and to-the-point explanations, feel free to use a few simple diagrams, charts, tables, or other graphic aids to get the point across with minimum paperwork.

And while we're on the subject of perfecting the deal, let's return to the broader picture of added value negotiating and remind ourselves not to be tempted to use the same kinds of postnegotiation trickery to which others often resort. Make the agreement cover exactly what you negotiated, no more and no less. Don't slip in provisions that were not discussed.

Expressed another way, make sure that the negotiating process covers all of the key elements of the deal and allows for the fine points you need to cover in the agreement. Then you won't be making up anything outside the scope of the discussions.

Everything said in this chapter deals with ways to put the spirit of added value negotiating into action and to make it a practical reality. Of course, not all negotiations will go smoothly. Not all will involve a counterpart who believes in the spirit of added value. There are still bulldogs and foxes in the world, and you can't convert them all. The deer may still sometimes get nervous and bolt on you, and we know that bulldogs can shift their behavior and act like foxes when it suits their purposes.

Yet, through all of the swings and roundabouts involved in the process, you will find the process itself to be your best friend. If you maintain the ethical stance of added value negotiating, work hard to build and maintain empathy, use openness and transparency to support the search for value, and advocate your own interests fairly and assertively, you will build better deals than with the traditional methods of negotiating from fixed positions.

Even in the worst of cases, you can do no worse than fall back to the conventional power game, but we believe that the more experience you have with the added value approach, the less you will need or want to resort to the old way. You'll become spoiled by the success of added value negotiating, and you'll hold yourself to a higher ethical standard in dealing with others. Who knows? Maybe some of it will rub off on them, too.

Chapter Nine

Some Final Thoughts on Negotiating

"Have you noticed ethics creeping into some of these deals lately?"

Drawing by H. Martin; © 1992 The New Yorker Magazine, Inc.

RECAPPING WHAT WE'VE LEARNED

Here are some simple ground rules to keep in mind as you use the added value negotiating method. They'll help you stay focused on the steps that make up the process and give you more confidence in your ability to use it as an effective negotiating tool.

1. Never make just one offer; always create at least two deals, and preferably more.
2. Listen carefully; understand the other party's interests clearly.
3. Don't personalize or emotionalize the process.
4. Take confidence in your veto power; you can always say no.
5. Trust the process; beware of shortcuts.
6. Don't expect perfect results every time. Some negotiating sessions will go more smoothly than others.
7. Model openness and compliance and act as if you expect the other party to do the same.
8. No piecemeal negotiating; work from the big picture, not one item at a time.
9. No power ploys, dirty tricks, or other manipulative traps or tactics.
10. No cherry-picking—each deal stands or falls on its own merits. Don't allow the other party to pick the best parts from all the deals in order to make a new one.

As with most things, the more you practice the more comfortable you'll feel using AVN when you sit down to negotiate. You may discover many more opportunities to use it than you first thought.

HELPING OTHERS NEGOTIATE SUCCESSFULLY

Added value negotiating can work especially well in the hands of a neutral third party who has been chosen by the principals to help them arrive at a deal. Here are some things to think about when you have occasion to serve in such a role:

Don't take sides. Both parties must see you as working to help them serve their interests. Even if one of them is not as easy to work with as the other, you still need to maintain an unbiased stance. Eventually, each of them will have to take responsibility for the deal that meets their needs as they see them. You can advise, suggest, and recommend, but in the end your best role is like that of a catalyst in a chemical reaction: you help the reaction along but you do not control it.

Maintain empathy. Be a skillful diplomat. Pay attention to the pattern of communication between the parties. Are they open and candid with each other? Do they share critical information? Do they project a cooperative attitude rather than a competitive one? What can you do to influence them in the direction of a cooperative search for value?

Work the process. Use all five steps in the AVN process. Don't be tempted to take shortcuts or to take a piece from here and a piece from there. Resist with all your might the tendencies of one or more parties to shortcut the process with offers and counteroffers. Encourage them to put the cards on the table and make their interests clear. Be sure you have a solid definition of the interests on both sides before you proceed to options. Do a good job of identifying the elements of value and the options for combining them before you begin to work with deal packages.

Resist the temptation to slap together one "best" deal and sell it to them. Develop multiple deal packages that offer various appeals and help them evaluate them against their interests. In short, stay with the process all the way, and you'll always know where you are.

Be thorough. Don't get lazy when it comes to the basic work of the process. Be willing to do some homework in identifying the elements of value. It may be worthwhile to get out your pencil, paper, and calculator—or even your computer—to figure out the relative value of certain options, so the parties can consider them intelligently. Help them analyze each of the deal packages thoroughly, until they are satisfied they understand each one in terms of the value it offers.

Be patient. Many times it won't be easy to arrive at a successful deal, and sometimes it won't even be possible. You must have a realistic attitude about the people involved, their quirks and biases, and the degree to which they can buy into the ethical stance of added value negotiating. The parties always have the option to fall back to the conventional pushing contest, but the AVN method offers the hope of leading them to a better deal, and one about which they can all feel better. Sometimes the best contribution of an outsider is simply to keep nudging them in the right direction, and to keep reminding them about the benefits of a focus on added value. Sometimes you'll end up with more lumps than any of the negotiating parties, but maybe that's part of your contribution.

USING AVN FOR CONFLICT RESOLUTION

People who are experts in conflict resolution, whether they are working with feuding married couples, with feuding neighbors, with neighborhoods feuding with police, with departments feuding inside an organization, with feuding organizations, or with feuding countries, all recognize that it is a form of negotiation. When two parties have been locked for a long time in a pattern of hostile action and counteraction, they are desperately in need of a new way of looking at things. The AVN method has the ingredients for resolving conflicts at all kinds of levels, because it can bring about the very shift in context and perspective that people need.

The protagonists in a conflict situation may not see themselves as in need of negotiation. Each tends to see the other as guilty of some disreputable behavior, and each tends to see his or her own behavior as simply a pattern of response to the bad behavior of the other. Turn this lopsided perception around both ways and it becomes symmetrical. Each is the victim of the other's transgressions. Each successive counterattack looks to the other party like a new attack, itself deserving of a reply in kind or, preferably, in greater measure.

A husband and wife have been fighting for so long about the same things that their fights are all basically reruns. Neither says anything new. Neither seeks anything different from the other. Neither offers anything of value to the other in exchange for the desired change in behavior.

Two corporate departments have been exchanging the same accusations of selfishness and unwillingness to cooperate for so long that the accusations are fully discounted by each of the accused. Their mind-sets have solidified around a position that reduces to "They're never going to change, and I don't *need* to change." Again, the perceptions are fully reciprocal. Each is innocent and the other is guilty.

Two political parties have been at war for so long that the mere idea of cooperation between them seems strange and somehow unnatural. Each blames the other for the country's failures. The party in power blames the opposition for thwarting its aims. The party in opposition blames the party in power for everything imaginable.

The Israelis and their Arab neighbors have been fighting for so long that nobody knows what started it, or even what it's really about. Of course, each of the factions can explain the "real" causes of the conflict—the evil behavior of the others. They can explain it, that is, to their own satisfaction, although not nearly to the satisfaction of the accused.

For conflicts like these to get resolved, at least partially, something has to happen to create a new context for their interaction. This might be the arrival of some common enemy, or some form of tragedy that befalls them both and makes them mutually dependent, or the intervention of some skillful third party that helps them redirect their energies away from their differences and more toward their possibilities.

Let's see how the AVN method can work as a technique for conflict resolution between two parties who are in strife. The basic steps in conflict resolution are roughly the same as in added value negotiating, with some extra attention paid to the problem of empathy:

1. Get the emotional temperature down. Seek a preliminary agreement between the parties that they will eliminate the posturing that is intensifying the conflict. They may not yet agree on the overall behaviors that are appropriate, but get them to agree that name-calling, criticizing, and fault-finding are temporarily suspended. This can create a temporary cease-fire, which prepares the way for meaningful discussions.

2. Redirect attention from behaviors to interests. Ask the parties to agree not to discuss each other's behavior for the time being, but to simply focus on clarifying their individual interests and communicating them in simple, nonjudgmental terms. This is the first step of the AVN model: clarifying interests. At this point, if you're just a bit lucky, the two parties may show some indication of willingness to entertain a different way of relating to each other and a willingness to discuss their interactions in terms of the interests they are trying to serve.

3. Add options to the behavioral repertoire. Help the parties identify individual and joint actions they could take that could begin serving some of their needs better. Try to identify behaviors that they would both be willing to refrain from, such as name-calling, accusing, withholding information, and so on. This is the second step of the AVN process: identifying options.

4. Form a consensus around new key behaviors. This can be a combination of steps three and four of the AVN method, that is, designing alternative deal packages and evaluating them cooperatively. In many conflict situations, it may be more convenient to formulate just one preferable deal, especially if the parties show signs of movement toward consensus. However, some conflict situations may be so complex that developing several possible deals may improve the quality of the dialogue, reduce interpersonal tension, and keep both parties in their individual comfort zones.

5. Define a new pattern for the relationship. Bring the agreement to specific terms that spell out how each of the parties agrees to behave. Get formal agreement and put the agreement on paper in plain language, even if it's only a few handwritten paragraphs. Get a commitment for a trial period to see how well the new arrangement will work.

Can you picture this five-step process of conflict resolution, which is really the AVN process with behavior as the focus of value, working in various conflict situations? Between a husband and wife? Within a troubled family? Between two departments? Between two business partners? Between two countries or political factions?

Think about each of the situations and imagine some of the behaviors that might be involved. How might the parties conceive their interests? What kinds of behavioral options might meet those interests?

Think about a conflict situation you might be experiencing on a personal basis. Can the AVN reasoning process apply in your situation or is yours somehow different? Recognize that it's usually easier to be objective and open-minded about resolving somebody else's conflict than about your own. Yet the same approach can make sense for you, too. If you find yourself involved in a particularly difficult conflict situation, you might want to consider asking a neutral but understanding third party to help you. If your counterpart in the conflict will accept such assistance, you may find the process surprisingly successful.

DIVORCE: THE MOST PERSONAL OF ALL NEGOTIATIONS

Divorce has probably caused more animosity, stress, anxiety, frustration, and gray hair than any other kind of negotiation—if, indeed, we can even call it a negotiation.

In the Western countries, and especially in the United States, divorce is becoming more and more common. By some measures, especially considering the changes in divorce law, it is becoming somewhat more humane, but it still has a long way to go to become a process in which fairly amicable feelings between the parties are the norm.

For many troubled relationships, a divorce proceeding is the finishing blow, the coup de grace without the grace. When two people decide to end their formal marital relationship, they may not hate each other, but the chances are fairly high that they will by the time they finish with the divorce, especially if there is a lawyer involved, and almost certainly if there are two lawyers involved.

Added value negotiating offers an important possibility for making divorce less of an adversarial proceeding and more of a joint search for value as two people go their separate ways. If the two are still able to communicate in a fairly civil manner, it can help them through the difficult personal negotiation that deals with everything that has been basic to their lives together.

If they are not on speaking terms, a neutral third party can use the AVN method to help them avoid combat, keep the emotional temperature at a minimum, and work things out fairly objectively.

One reason why so many divorces involve hard feelings is the very adversarial nature of the traditional process by which both sides interpose lawyers as advocates between themselves. By definition, a lawyer cannot represent both parties. The best one can hope for is to have one lawyer, who represents one party, come up with a settlement the other party can live with. If this works, there need be no real litigation.

Unfortunately, too many divorce lawyers yield to the temptation to push the matter into litigation by attacking the unrepresented party with an aggressively unbalanced offer, which in turn forces that person to seek representation. When there are two lawyers involved, each can generate higher fees than the one could have in a one-sided case. This situation is a natural for combat, because both parties are likely to be in a highly disturbed and unstable emotional state, and, therefore, highly reactive to the kinds of threats and insults so common to such proceedings.

There is a growing trend in some countries, particularly in the United States, to use mediators as neutral third parties instead of lawyers who advocate each side. This is an enormously promising trend. The evidence indicates that mediated settlements stick far more reliably than court-ordered settlements, that is, far fewer of them end up back in court. Mediated divorces tend to be less costly than lawyer-managed divorces and far less costly than highly contentious litigated settlements.

Further, an added value negotiating approach to the settlement can offer all sorts of creative options for dividing assets in ways that meet the interests of both parties more effectively. For example, rather than sell the house immediately, possibly in unfavorable economic times, the couple could consider various approaches to timing, division of equity, cash versus equity, and continuous sharing of equity for a period of time.

Empathy is a critical key to this type of settlement. If the parties involved, or their neutral intermediary, can maintain a state of reasonable empathy, openness, and trust—which the AVN method makes easier because of its focus on value and not on combat—they are much more likely to reach a balanced agreement in a shorter period of time. Further, many couples find that they are able to reduce their feelings of anger and animosity as they see themselves cooperating in the process.

Mediation will probably become a much more popular avenue for divorce and possibly for many other aspects of negotiation. In the United States, there is an Academy of Family Mediators located in Eugene, Oregon. Other states are developing local associations as well.

Of course, it might make just as much sense to focus on added value negotiating earlier in the process, that is, as two people approach marriage. Love can't afford to be blind anymore. People need to understand themselves and one another before they enter into important ventures such as marriages.

Marriage, for most people, is a legal contract with unspecified terms. The terms get specified only when you try to break the contract. It is far better for two people to work out the critical elements of value in their relationship before they enter into it, including provisions for ending the relationship if that becomes necessary. Paradoxically, the better defined the relationship and the better people stick to their agreement, the less likely it may be to fail.

CAN AVN WORK BETWEEN NATIONS?

Is it hopelessly idealistic, unrealistic, and naive to think that nations with a history of hostility, conflict, and warfare can relate to one another from the ethical stance of added value negotiating? There are a few hopeful signs, but we have to admit the record so far isn't encouraging.

The United States and the former Soviet Union spent some 40 years locked in a Cold War of threats and counterthreats that cost both of them dearly and eventually sank the economy of the latter. As mentioned previously, there is a strange reciprocal psychology of mutual aggression and conflict. Each justifies its view of the other as the aggressor and justifies its own behavior as merely a natural and sensible reaction to aggression.

American citizens were conditioned by their political leaders to see the Soviets as the original dangerous aggressors, yet few Americans ever wondered how the Soviets viewed American behavior. Immediately following World War II, which the United States ended by dropping atomic bombs on Japan, the United States developed and deployed the B-52 long-range bomber. This was a delivery system, capable of aerial refueling, with no other possible mission than to drop atomic bombs on the Soviet Union. What were the Soviets supposed to think?

The Americans soon followed up the B-52 with the Intercontinental Ballistic Missile, or ICBM, another device with no other plausible purpose than to deliver warheads—these nuclear rather than just atomic— on the Soviet Union. Soon thereafter came the development of the submarine-launched nuclear missile. The United States then had a three-pronged nuclear capability, the infamous triad, aimed at the Soviet Union. What were the Soviets supposed to think?

At the close of his administration as president of the United States, Dwight Eisenhower warned his fellow countrymen of the increasing power of the military-industrial complex, a growing entity with a commercial and political stake in the continuation of the tensions of the Cold War. For their part, the Soviets had their own political factions and a communist view of their destiny as world leaders that fed the conflict as well. Within a few years after the close of World War II, the conflict between the United States and the Soviet Union was fully reciprocal and feeding on itself.

Israel and various Arab countries have been embroiled for centuries in a series of wars. Those animosities have been fully reciprocal for many years. Cultures in that part of the world tend to have a particularly vicious form of retaliation for what they perceive as unprovoked aggression. One must retaliate in kind and in extra measure. It's the Old Testament dictum of "an eye for an eye and a tooth for a tooth." In that state of affairs, everybody eventually winds up blind and toothless. Like two contentious children, each tries to make sure he gets a bit more than "even" by inflicting more damage on the other than he received.

Negotiations, if we can call them that, take place between these dedicated adversaries in the context of a continuous exchange of hostile acts. Arabs capture Israeli citizens and hold them hostage while supposedly negotiating political issues. Israelis destroy entire Palestinian villages while supposedly negotiating with them on issues of their political sovereignty. The government of Israel transports Israeli citizens into the occupied territories and subsidizes the building of their settlements while presumably negotiating about the status of those territories.

Trade wars have become a modern surrogate for warfare as a demonstration of national machismo. Various countries fire accusations at one

another, charging restrictive and unfair trade practices and slapping re-
taliatory tariffs and embargoes on one another's products.

Then, to add fuel to the feuds, journalists have had a long tradition of
concentrating on conflict in creating their products. The popular press
and electronic media often intensify conflict by highlighting it to the virtual exclusion of evidence of cooperation. War, worry, violence, and fear
sell soap; cooperation, collaboration, harmony, and peace do not sell
soap because they aren't good "news." A private slogan used by American journalists is "If it bleeds, it leads."

In the face of this discouraging evidence that testosterone is the most
influential chemical in international relationships, we have seen for
many years attempts to develop alternative methods of resolving differences. The Harvard Negotiation Project has contributed importantly to
the technology of conflict resolution in the Middle East and elsewhere.
Private nonprofit groups have worked to resolve individual issues, gain
the release of hostages, and focus attention on human rights problems.

On the international trade front, there have been notable attempts to
create an added value context for working out trade problems. Indeed,
the entire concept of the European Community has been to create an un-
precedented level of political and economic cooperation.

Some of the most skilled negotiators working today are beginning to
advocate more and more the ethical stance of added value. One of the big
problems with the mindset of negotiation up until now has been the accepted wisdom that negotiating is a difficult, confused, messy process,
and it just takes hard work and persistence. If we can get more people to
realize that by changing the psychological and social context of negotiating, such that it proceeds from interests, options, and added value,
there is a chance that more leaders of nations and political factions will
begin to see negotiating as more in their self-interest than fighting.

SHOULD WE TEACH NEGOTIATING
IN SCHOOLS?

If negotiating is such an important life skill, why do so many of us know
so little about it? Of course, we can ask the same question about many
of the topics and skills of the 21st-century life curriculum, and we'll get
the same answers. Most of our schools are dedicated to the pursuit of
irrelevance. The chances that a typical child will learn very much in a

classroom that will equip him or her for life in the new world is fairly remote. The child will learn plenty from his or her peers in the halls, in the bathroom, and on the playground, but not much anywhere else.

Children in the Western world learn many self-limiting and self-defeating attitudes during their growing-up years, which they spend the rest of their lives struggling to unlearn. One of those faulty attitudes is often an attitude about relative scarcity and abundance. When mom tells one kid to break the cookie in two and the other kid to choose his or her part, both kids get an unconscious message about scarcity. You have to divide the cookie and you won't get as much of it as you want. Furthermore, it's in your best interest to find a way to trick the other kid into getting the smaller piece of the cookie.

Almost all of the games and sports children learn to play give them the win-lose message: Somebody wins and everybody else loses. The grading system tells them the same thing. The IQ scores used to slot them into administrative categories tell them the same thing. Because there can only be one winner in most games, the majority of children are guaranteed a childhood of losing rather than winning. The phys-ed teacher chooses the biggest and most skillful kids for the team; the others get the message that they're not worthy.

We need to help our children learn the attitudes and belief systems of abundance, not of scarcity. We need to help them comprehend the idea that half a cookie isn't always the best you can do. We need to help them learn to solve problems cooperatively, to recognize that they can win by helping someone else win and to understand that there may be a bigger win in cooperating than there is in competing.

It's not too farfetched to visualize children at a fairly early age exposed to the ideas of cooperative problem solving and value creation. If the human reflexes of taking, holding, withholding, conserving, and defending can be reconditioned toward observing, listening, offering, sharing, and exchanging, we can help our children see themselves as capable problem solvers rather than defensive victims of coercion. Perhaps they will grow into a generation of leaders who create value and add value rather than fight and threaten and struggle.

This, we believe, is the promise of the added value philosophy of living, doing business, and negotiating.

Understanding

Your values are not my values;
Your thoughts are not my thoughts.
You have come here by a long and winding path,
*   as have I.*

Our paths may cross, but they are not the same path.
You believe as you do, you feel as you do, you react as you do,
Because you have travelled your own path.
And I have travelled mine.

If I can accept you and your values,
Your beliefs, and your reactions,
Respond to you as you are — not as I would like you to be;
If I can grant the sovereignty of your values
And you can grant the sovereignty of mine,
Then we have the beginning of understanding.

Bibliography

Fisher, Roger; William Ury; and Bruce Patton. *Getting to Yes*. 2nd ed. New York: Penguin Books, 1981.

Freund, James C. *Smart Negotiating*. New York: Simon & Schuster, 1992.

Fuller, George. *The Negotiator's Handbook*. New Jersey: Prentice Hall, 1991.

Ilich, John. "Principles of Negotiating." In *Executive Excellence Newsletter*, April 1990, pp. 10–11.

Karrass, Chester L. *Give & Take*. New York: Thomas Y. Crowell Publishers, 1974.

——— . *The Negotiating Game*. New York: Thomas Y. Crowell Publishers, 1970.

March, Robert M. *The Japanese Negotiator*. New York: Kondashsa International, 1988.

Nierenberg, Gerard I. *The Complete Negotiator*. New York: Nierenberg & Zeif Publishing, 1986.

Reck, Ross R.; and Brian G. Long. *The Win-Win Negotiator*. New York: Simon & Schuster, 1985.

Warschaw, Tessa. *Winning by Negotiation*. New York: McGraw Hill, 1980.

About the Authors

Karl Albrecht is a management consultant, speaker, researcher, and prolific author. During his 20-year career, he has established an impressive reputation for pioneering new ideas that contribute to greater organizational and individual effectiveness. He has written 18 books on various aspects of business including bestselling *Service America!*, *At America's Service*, *Service Within*, and *The Only Thing That Matters*. He is the most widely quoted authority, internationally, on the management of service quality. He is also chairman of The TQS Group, Inc., a Chicago-based consulting firm that implements his total quality service approach to business performance.

Steve Albrecht is the Director of Seminars for Albrecht Training & Development, a San Diego-based company specializing in negotiating, business writing, service management, and law enforcement training seminars. He is the author of six books and holds a bachelor of arts degree in English from the University of San Diego. He is nationally known for his written work on criminal justice issues. He designed the Added Value Negotiating seminar with his father, Karl Albrecht.

For more information about training in added value negotiating and other programs, please contact:

Albrecht Training & Development
2065 Arnold Way, Suite 103B
Alpine, CA 91901
(619) 445-4735

Index

Other Business One Irwin Books by Karl Albrecht . . .

Service America!
Doing Business in the New Economy
Karl Albrecht and Ron Zemke
More than 250,000 copies sold! This classic service primer shows you how to make service quality an imperative in your organization and increase your profits and customer loyalty! (203 pages)
ISBN: 0-87094-659-5

At America's Service
How Corporations Can Revolutionize the Way They Treat
Their Customers
Karl Albrecht
More than 50,000 copies sold! An essential guide that shows how to ensure that your customers return with repeat business! (240 pages)
ISBN: 1-55623-095-8

The Service Advantage
How to Identify and Fulfill Customer Needs
Karl Albrecht and Lawrence J. Bradford
This resource shows you how to understand your customers' wants, needs, attitudes, and buying tendencies to give your company a competitive advantage! (200 pages)
ISBN 1-55623-247-0

Service Within
Solving the Middle Management Leadership Crisis
Karl Albrecht
Mobilize your middle management team and deliver quality service within your organization! Albrecht shows how to increase cooperation between departments so that the entire organization works together more efficiently. (200 pages)
ISBN: 1-55623-353-1

Available at fine bookstores and libraries everywhere.